Wakefield Press

Finnenisms

Through more than 40 years in print journalism, David Sly has worked for the *News* and *Advertiser* in Adelaide, was editor of the *Adelaide Review*, been published in more than 50 Australian and International magazines as a freelance contributor, and is a graduate of the University of Adelaide / Le Cordon Bleu Gastronomy course. After initially focusing on music and entertainment, David also writes about many other consuming passions: food and wine, history, scientific research, comedy, snow skiing and travel.

FINNENISMS

Chris Finnen riffs on his 70 years of music

DAVID SLY

Wakefield Press

Wakefield Press
16 Rose Street
Mile End
South Australia 5031
www.wakefieldpress.com.au

First published 2024

Copyright © David Sly and Chris Finnen, 2024

All rights reserved. This book is copyright. Apart from any fair dealing for the purposes of private study, research, criticism or review, as permitted under the Copyright Act, no part may be reproduced without written permission. Enquiries should be addressed to the publisher.

Guitar photographs by Tony Lewis
All other photographs provided by Chris Finnen unless credited otherwise

Text designed and typeset by Jesse Pollard, Wakefield Press

ISBN 978 1 92304 264 3

 A catalogue record for this book is available from the National Library of Australia

 Wakefield Press thanks Coriole Vineyards for continued support

'This book is dedicated to my mother, Elizabeth Finnen
The kindest woman I have ever known.'

Chris Finnen

Contents

Foreword
by Matt Taylor   ix

Introduction   xi

Author's Note   xii

Chapter 1
Embarking on a new life   1

Chapter 2
Arriving ahead of time   8

Chapter 3
A blues record changed everything   16

Chapter 4
Earning the right to play an electric guitar   22

Chapter 5
All-night gigs in Melbourne   30

Chapter 6
Commencing a love affair with Adelaide   38

Chapter 7
The ever-changing, long-enduring Chris Finnen Band   56

Chapter 8
Open to all influences   68

Chapter 9
Folk and rock and blues and everything else   77

Chapter 10
The lessons learned from performing with others   87

Chapter 11
Parenthood — 102

Chapter 12
Tour . . . record . . . tour — 108

A final note . . .
by Jeff Lang — 127

Chris Finnen Discography — 129

'We've all been at the party when someone has
gone on and on and on, with nothing to say.
If you don't mean it, don't play it.'

Chris Finnen

Foreword
by Matt Taylor

They call it Stormy Monday but Tuesday's just the same in Finnenisms. He calls it Barramundy but Taylor or some other fish is just the same. Basically, these sayings that come from Chris Finnen go in one ear, you laugh, then they go straight out the other ear – and I've been hearing his witticisms for as long as I can remember. Actually, neither of us can remember when or how we first met, but it has been at least 40 years that I've been suffering the Finnenisms, while he's suffered my constant Phil-osyphising, and we both know that good music and good humour will keep us brothers for life.

In the 1980s, we formed The Matt Taylor band featuring Chris Finnen. He moved over to Perth and we'd play the pub circuit four nights a week, then tour all over Australia. My first warning to Chris was about our bass player Roy Daniel. 'Whatever you do, don't get involved in any of Roy's practical jokes.' But, of course he did, and it ended with large water pistols, balloon water bombs and full buckets of water balanced atop motel doors. Fond memories, for sure.

We wrote a few songs together for the *Always Land on Your Feet* album, and that's when I learned that Chris – along with the likes of Phil Manning – can start a riff, and before you know it, we're working on a brand-new song. Jamming with one of Chris's Adelaide bands at the KoKlub on Hindley St in Adelaide many years later, I got the idea for *Who is McGoo* for my *Walls to McGoo* album. The creative energy that surrounds this man at every gig provides a place where you can always try new things. We're not playing note-perfect pop music in Chain; we're venturing past the edge. Yeah, sometimes we may fall flat but mostly your fellow musicians get inspired to take the audience to a place of wonder – and when they're listening to Chris's sublime solos, to experience a sense of awe.

I'm amazed sometimes when I talk to South Australians who haven't heard of Chris Finnen. OK, we live in a world crammed with TV talent shows where the notion of creativity is to reproduce a well-known song and be judged by whether it's identical or not, instead of reaching for true inspiration. I understand that if those shows insisted on original new music, nobody would probably tune in. But those people are the ones missing out, because they don't know about someone like Finnen. Chris is an artist in the most creative sense. He can take you on an unpredictable journey which turns into a truly memorable musical experience – but first you must make the effort to want to go there with him.

One of the joys of my life is visiting Adelaide and playing music with Chris, who is a true master of his Art. He's sensitive to the feelings of others, creative in all his actions – but yes, he does have rather questionable dress sense. And there's also those endless Finnenisms. Well, it all still adds up to a great time had by all.

Matt Taylor,
February 2024

Introduction

The world of music exists for me on a constant basis. Every day I'm listening to it, thinking about it, teaching it, committing to daily practice, playing it wherever possible and sharing it with other people. I can't walk to the shops or get on board a train without music constantly living inside my head.

I've been told that I'm married to my music, and – fair enough – I have to admit it's the most successful marriage I've had in my life.

Guitar, voice and percussion have become my chosen medium for self-expression. They offer a link to spirituality, contentment and great joy, and provide me with a huge sense of fulfillment, creativity and purpose.

I've had an ongoing love affair with the guitar for more than five decades, and it has endured everything through my life. This magnificent instrument has been a catalyst for my education, friendships, travel and an ever-expanding knowledge of ethno-musicality, anthropology and emotional development that steers me through our ever-changing world.

Music always gives back and it always grows. I can only thank my lucky stars that it has been my chosen mode for expressing the richness of life.

Chris Finnen,
24 December 2023

Author's Note

When Chris approached me with the idea of writing his story, he presented a series of sheets on which he had carefully catalogued key moments in his life. They captured all the essential wit, wisdom and Finnenisms that define Mr Finnen, and so they have been included as he wrote them.

But there was much more to tell. Long conversations between us, and with key people in his life and music, drew out more essential detail. My journalism instincts kicked in, and a narrative was constructed to complement Chris's written passages and snatches of song lyrics.

Just as Chris has many guitars, there is a chorus of voices featured in this book – but it begins with Chris recalling the event that changed and shaped his life, being his passage from England to Australia aboard *Ellinis* in January 1967.

David Sly

Chapter 1
Embarking on a new life

13 January, 1967: Somehow that bleak, grey Sussex sky managed to reach the floor. Perhaps the bleakness was magnified by my 14-year-old consciousness, struggling with the idea of leaving behind all that I had grown up with and known in life so far.

Still, excitement prevailed. I was embarking on a trip to Australia. The Land Down Under. The great antipodean continent. The island far away, on the other side of the world.

On this day of departure, however, the sledgehammer of reality hit me. My family said goodbye to life-long friends. My dear younger sister was heartbroken at having to leave behind her beloved dog. There were suitcases and bags piled high, plus anticipation and thoughts of adventure all swirling around in my teenage brain as I prepared to go on a global ride.

During our family's train journey from home to London, I managed one last fleeting look at my beloved Gatwick Airport, where so many of my childhood hours had been spent blissfully observing some of the great moments in aviation history – namely the transition period from piston (radial) engines to turboprop and then onto jet engines.

London really marked the start of our great southern journey. We boarded a train full of hopeful migrants heading for the Southampton docks, which was home to the greatest ocean liners of the day. Those dockside were the great Cunard ships, which had merged with the infamous White Star Line, plus P&O Line, Union Castle, Blue Funnel, Shaw Saville, Canadian Pacific and the United States Line, just to name a few. Even the great Titanic had left from these docks 52 years earlier.

This was happening in the days when great ships were feminine and beautiful, and they didn't look like car parks with funnels stuck on top. Our ship was the Chandris Shipping Line's twin-funnel *Ellinis*. Her gleaming white hull was being loaded with a constant stream of people and luggage for the great journey ahead. At 9.30pm, we looked over the railings into the grey, churning water as the dockside filled with many emotional people. Streamers were flying. The wind was in my hair and my heart was beating faster, because our adventure had truly started.

We were post-war new Elizabethans, heading for a new land and leaving behind the old, for whatever may lay ahead. We had dreams of a bright new future.

Only now do I realise how difficult this must have been for my parents. I can only imagine how hard it must have been to leave behind their history, their family roots and their friends in a quest to provide a better life for themselves and their children.

Fortunately, they were not alone. Aunty Mary, Uncle Bob and my two cousins, Julie and Debbie, were part of this great family unit that had embarked on the same adventure. The voyage gave us all plenty of time to contemplate, plan, relax and discover the world, as we slowly traversed thousands of miles of ocean under wide open skies.

During our first morning at sea, there was a lifeboat drill for all passengers and crew. We lined up at our appointed boat station, and mum found a small child wandering about, lost and upset. She brought the child to the boat station, and earned the praise of the crew, but she was agitated by the lax attitude of the absent parents. 'We're supposed to pretend this is a real emergency,' she declared.

Our ship arrived at Flushing, a port in Holland, to pick up Dutch passengers. There were lots of ships in this busy port and I wish I could have gone ashore for a look around. Instead, we went to the ship's cinema that evening to watch *McHale's Navy Joins the Air Force.*

We steamed through the Bay of Biscay, continued past the rock of Gibraltar and headed into the Mediterranean. The ship was buzzed at low-level by a Dutch Navy Lockheed Neptune on surveillance exercises. It reminded me just how much I love aviation.

On January 20, we arrived in Piraeus, Greece, which was our ship's home port. We were taken on a sightseeing tour around Athens, with the highlight being a visit to the Acropolis. Such unbelievable architecture, and an incredible insight of an ancient culture. It was almost too much for young Chris to contemplate when he turned in that night.

The ship moored in the harbour overnight and departed early the next morning, heading for Port Said in Egypt. I was so eagerly awaiting our arrival in the Suez Canal. In Port Said, I was introduced to the methodology of Arabic trading. I saw merchants shimmying up ropes, their craniums covered with what looked like tea towels, bearing suitcases with such exotic Arabic names as Jock McGregor, Paddy O'Grady and Angus McDuff. The water was filled with many little boats containing people plying their trade, and it was all so exotic for a 14-year-old boy from Sussex. We managed to disembark the ship via a floating platform of wooden pontoons that had been strung together. We exited though a door located low in the ship's hull, which served to emphasise the ship's gigantic scale. From ground level, its gleaming hull looked absolutely huge.

Once on land, we proceeded down a narrow Egyptian street, with buses rushing past that had as many people on the roof and clinging to the outside of the vehicle as there were internally accommodated. The place was busy – and if it wasn't a mecca for spirituality, then it was certainly a mecca for flies and for squalid poverty – but, ahh, what an atmosphere!

Upon reboarding our ship, we noticed that great emphasis had been placed on cabin security, and warnings were given in the ship's newspaper to anyone who had purchased souvenir toy camels. They had been stuffed with very unhygienic bits of material and were certain to be confiscated by customs officials immediately upon landing in Australia.

Once we started traversing the great Suez Canal, I learned that ships can only travel in one direction – rather like South Australian motorways of the early 2000s. Our canal voyage was therefore interrupted, and we spent many hours at anchor in the Bitter Lakes to make room for ships travelling in the opposite direction. Still, there was beautiful sunshine, and I had plenty of time to play my guitar and enjoy the laidback life aboard ship. The great and much larger P&O liner *Canberra* was at rest behind us. I knew that because she was so much faster and newer than our ship, she would beat us across the Indian Ocean and reach Australia ahead of us.

Still, *Ellinis* (which means 'Greek maiden') was a beautiful ship. It was a One Class ship that had been given a complete refit over six passenger decks by Chandris Lines, modified to service the Australian migrant trade, and we were aboard its 18th southbound voyage. It was originally built in 1933 as *Lurline*, designed for Hawaiian cruises with the Matson Line, and many of her Hawaiian appointments remained on board, including the Waikiki and Coral dining rooms, the Veranda Ballroom, Outrigger Bar, Palm Cinema and Polynesian Room. Her gross tonnage was 18,564 tonnes, she was 642 feet long (196 metres) and 79 feet wide (24 metres), and had a service speed of 22 knots. Her captain on our journey was J. Ikiadis.

At last, we departed Bitter Lakes at 8.15pm on 23 January, bound for Aden and feeling excited about getting closer to Australia. I was also feeling glad to be on holiday from school, and looking forward to crossing the Equator.

On 24 January, my mum turned 38, as we steamed ever onward through the Red Sea. The waves didn't part for us, but the ship's band came to our table and played Happy Birthday for mum, and our waiter, Arris Adamopolis, resplendent in his wine-red uniform, was his usual charming self, tending to every detail for the special dinner with great care. I was dressed for dinner and was grateful that, at the age of 14, I was a member of the adult dining room, along with mum, dad, Auntie Mary and Uncle Bob – while my younger sister and two cousins had to eat during the earlier children's dining sessions.

At about 4pm on January 26, our ship arrived in Aden, but I had to stay on board due to political unrest. There was a strong military presence at the docks, so the adults were allowed ashore for a short while, and mum and dad returned to present me with a double-ended hand drum. I immediately proceeded to start practising hand percussion, which launched my never-ending love affair with drums and percussion. Unfortunately, that drum was confiscated by customs officials once we landed in Australia, all in the name of bio-security. There were no gamma ray treatments of animal hide drums skins back then.

By 11.10pm, we had departed Aden and started our journey across the great Indian Ocean, bound for Fremantle.

On January 29, we crossed the Equator, marked by a Crossing the Line ceremony featuring King Neptune and all his friends around the ship's swimming pool. However, when it came time for the Captain's Crossing the Line Cocktail Party, I couldn't attend because I was too young. Blast. I only wish I was older! Instead, I went to a cabin party with a friend from my dining table – Roland Idris Lloyd, a Welshman. And that was a super party. There were bikini-clad girls, Foster's Lager and The Beatles' *Revolver* album on the record player, *Tomorrow Never Knows* blasting from the speakers. Wow! Beer, crumpet, music and psychedelia all in one afternoon whilst at sea.

During this portion of the journey, we didn't sight land for 12 days – but we did see several schools of flying fish, which delighted my cousin Debbie. I started thinking about Christopher Columbus, Captain Cook and Charles Darwin at sea in their tiny little ships, negotiating rough seas and very big waves. And before I knew it, our ship was on the other side of the world and getting closer to Australia with every passing day.

On February 7, 1967, we arrived at the port of Fremantle, Western Australia. The sky was blue, the sun was bright. There were people on the quayside and jellyfish in the water. We went ashore and our feet touched Australian soil for the first time, although my body still retained the pitching and rolling motion of the ship. We were taken on a quick tour of King's

Park, and immediately noticed the flora and fauna being so very different from England. We then went to a cafe for beans on toast and cups of tea. 'At last – real milk,' we declared.

I will return to Perth many years later, but at this time my family returned to the ship for our final leg of the journey – to Melbourne. I was standing alone on the deck and had a strange, overwhelming experience that I still don't quite understand. While gazing at the beautiful blue sea and sky, my whole being filled with distant, ethereal, heavenly music. Time stood still and all I could do was surrender to the intensity of this incredibly strong feeling. I kept it all to myself, and didn't dare tell mum or dad unless they thought I was a looney.

Now, as I enter my 70th year, I get transported straight back as I recall that surreal, special moment when I could hear distant music from afar. If only I knew back then what this moment would come to signify in my life later on . . .

We had a fantastic Welcome to Australia dinner onboard the ship. The special dessert was Bombe Alaska. All the lights in the dining room were dimmed and the ship's waiters entered, carrying aloft the spectacular flaming trays of delicious dessert.

Over the next few days, as we crossed the Great Australian Bight on our way to Melbourne, the excitement of approaching our new home was steadily building. I recall my first taste of Australian fruit onboard the ship. It was an orange but it looked to me like a grapefruit, because it was so much larger than any orange I had ever seen before. It was firm, succulent and juicy, with the mysterious word Mildura stamped in blue ink on its skin.

This was my first taste of many astounding things that I would find in Australia, and would shape my life. It was a revelation to me. I was excited but naïve – and so much more lay ahead.

Chapter 2
Arriving ahead of time

Christopher James Finnen was born in Redhill Hospital, Surrey, England – three months premature – on Christmas Eve 1952, and the early arrival affected his sight, which would be such a decisive factor in his life.

Baby Chris weighed only 3 pounds, so he was placed in a humidicrib incubator for the first three months of his life, but during that time he was given too much oxygen which affected his eye development. It resulted in Chris having no vision in his right eye and a degenerative condition in his left eye.

While his vision was problematic, Chris says he never felt that he faced insurmountable hurdles as a child. 'I really didn't think about it until I was about 14,' he says. 'The doctor I went to simply explained that I had tunnel vision. My parents never gave me a prognosis. It just wasn't talked about.'

Chris says he didn't have special concessions through his childhood, but he found crossing roads difficult, and would ask for an adult to give him assistance – especially crossing the A23 that ran through his home town of Crawley, being the main road between London and Brighton.

'It made me more determined to achieve things, in some ways,' he says. 'I knew I had only partial vision. Of course, there were things I could not see, but there were some things that I could see that other people overlooked. I suppose I began to see things in my own way.'

Family life in the Finnen family's red-brick, semi-detached home in Crawley, West Sussex (about 45 kilometres south of London) was simple and happy. Both parents worked, though they never spoke much about their lives to their children. Chris's father, Jim (more commonly known as Jock, reflecting his Scottish heritage), worked in coal mines during World War Two but then went to London, where his mother worked as a costume designer. Consequently, from 1946, Jim worked in the theatre, as a chauffeur and valet for many star performers – including Robert Morley, Stuart Grainger, Tony Hancock and he even befriended America's Danny Kaye.

Chris's mother, Elizabeth, who hailed from Newcastle, worked part-time as a window dresser in a local haberdashery store, and she was up for the occasional prank. 'She'd come home from work and greet me by shaking my hand, but she'd placed a pig's trotter from the local butcher at the end of her sleeve, and the trotter would come off in my hand,' remembers Chris, 'and we'd both fall about laughing.'

This rather particular Finnen brand of humour had been forged from listening to the wireless. The family would gather to listen to programs featuring The Goons, *Round the Horne*, and especially Tony Hancock. 'Hancock was masterful for the timing of the pause, and the art of making the listener wait for what was going to be delivered,' says Chris. This taste for goofy humour also shaped Chris's appetite for early TV programs, such as *The Telegoons*, a short-lived program from 1962 to 1964, featuring puppets that performed to the voices of Peter Sellars and Spike Milligan.

The Finnen family – which included Chris's younger sister Sue, who is three years his junior – would also gather around the kitchen table each evening for meals; traditional English fare that largely focused on over-boiled vegetables and a joint of mutton for the Sunday roast dinner. There were kippers and porridge for breakfast, although proud

Finnenisms

Scotsman Jim Finnen would scowl disapprovingly in the direction of young Chris when he defiled the simple purity of his morning porridge by drizzling a large quantity of Lyle's Golden Syrup on top of the boiled oats.

The family also took annual holidays to the north, riding the train to Newcastle, to visit Elizabeth Finnen's mother (her father had died young). Chris remembers going to King's Cross Station in 1962 ('leaving from the same platforms where they shot the *Harry Potter* movie scenes featuring the Hogwarts Express') and boarding the north-bound train pulled by a streamlined Mallard steam engine. 'I used to love travelling along that line. The scenery was magnificent and the thrill of being on that steam train was a great adventure.'

MEMORIES OF A NORTHUMBRIAN JOURNEY
Boarding the overnight train from London to Newcastle, it struck me that King's Cross Station was built in 1852, which is exactly 100 years before I was born. We took this journey during the last days of steam, and the engine pulling our train was one of Sir Nigel Gresley's Class A4 Mallards with the beautiful sloping front (this model had broken the speed record for steam engines in 1938, clocking an impressive 126mph). It was a wondrous sight to behold, along with the maroon coaches which had smoke-stained windows, wood-panelled compartments and corridors to stretch your legs in. For a 10-year-old boy, it was a very exciting journey to visit Nanny Johnson and my mum's home town. I loved Nanny Johnson's thick Geordie accent, her big heart, her tough love and her paisley apron.

There were sights to behold all along the train line. At Darlington Station, I saw Locomotive No 1 perched up on a plinth – it was the first locomotive to run on a public railway, along the Stockton and Darlington line. Further along I saw the Durham viaduct plus the city's magnificent castle and

> cathedral. Then, in Newcastle, we pulled into Central Station, the largest railway junction in Britain. I saw the five bridges of the Tyne, and an old gasometer towering above the old houses. It was a city on the brink of change, experiencing the final days of heavy industry, but I got to see the steam engines shunting coal wagons and big steam ships on the docks. The family took a train down to Whitely Bay, visiting the Spanish City concert hall, tea rooms and fun fair, and we had large jars of mussels in vinegar. I consumed one of them all by myself. Yummy.

Once he arrived in Newcastle, Chris heard folk music being played in his relatives' homes, especially songs about coal miners. 'I came to realise straight away that folk music was the true and unadorned voice of the people. Those songs told the stories of all our families.' He was also thrilled to hear the northern accent in songs and in conversation. The mystery of the Geordie dialect was both baffling and provided a delightful music to his ears. 'My grandmother would say to me "gan doon scullery takwa beit" which meant that I should head into the kitchen for lunch. She spoke so quickly that the words came at a blur, but I loved it. It sounded so interesting – and so very musical.'

Scotland was another a destination for Finnen family holidays, to connect with Jim 'Jock' Finnen's homeland.

> Dad was very proud of his Scottish heritage, so we took many family trips to Scotland. One of these took us across the famous Queensbury Passage in 1962, involving a trip across the Firth of Forth on a car ferry. This huge river was spanned by the magnificent cantilevered Forth Rail Bridge, built from 51,000 tons of steel, which opened in March 1890 and was 1.75 miles long, rising 361 feet above the water. Only two years after we visited, the ferry service ceased when the Forth Road Suspension Bridge opened to carry vehicle traffic. Our holiday

> included a visit to Leuchars RAF Air Base at St Andrews, where we saw all sorts of planes doing low and loud 'hedge-hopping' flights, and we went on to beautiful Edinburgh. I remember visiting Princess Street, the floral clock, the Scott memorial, and the daily firing of the one o'clock gun from Edinburgh Castle. What a thunderous boom!

On other trips to Scotland, Chris fondly remembers his father skimming flat rocks across the still, dark waters of Loch Lamond; of standing next to the stumps of the old Tay Bridge, which had collapsed in a wild gale in December 1887, taking a trainload of 76 passengers to their deaths in the River Tay; and feeling the heavy moss, quartzite and stone in the undulating Roman remains of Hadrian's Wall.

In 1964, Chris embarked on an adventure in a Land Rover with the Wildlife rangers, touring the Lake District area in Cumbria ('one of the most beautiful places I have ever been to, with such lush greenery and picturesque small villages') before heading into Scotland and travelling to the northern tip of the country, reaching the remote and rugged mountain region of Sutherland.

> On our approach to Lochinver, the peaks of Canisp, Suilven and Cul Mor stood out like ancient ghostly sentinels amid the fields of coarse heather and stone. We were taken by a wooden boat over to the beautiful Handa Island, where we stayed in a one-room stone cottage with wooden bunk beds, and we burned peat on the fire for warmth. The island is mostly grass, bracken and towering rocks – one being a sheer-faced rocky plinth rising from the ocean that served as a bird sanctuary for fulmars, gannets, great skuas, Arctic skuas, puffins, guillemots, kittiwakes, gulls, terns and cormorants. There were also seals and otters in the water. It was an unforgettable experience to be on that isolated, uninhabited island for a week, which was as far north as I had ever been.

I also remember Cumbria as being a very special place. We stayed at a youth camp in Langdale Pikes and I can vividly remember climbing the 2,403 foot-high Harrison Stickle, and the exhilarating feeling of sitting among moss-covered rocks on the peak, in the middle of thick, damp clouds. I could see for miles around with the aid of my trusty telescope, and considering my limited eyesight, I considered that quite an achievement. I also remember that the tiny roads had hairpin bends and gradients steeper than 20%. We passed Blea Tarn, Little Langdale, Kirkstone Pass with its red scree, and Raven Crag, travelling on a minor road known as The Struggle because it was unusable in bad weather. We managed to make it to the town of Ambleside, at the head of Lake Windermere (closely associated with *Beatrix Potter* books and the poet William Wordsworth). We visited Keswick, and I loved its church in the main street. A market charter had been granted to this place by King Edward 1 in 1276, and it remains a vibrant market town, selling such local culinary treats as white and brown Kendal Mint Cake. We went to Coniston Water, where Donald Campbell broke the world speed record in his jet-powered boat Bluebird, and who tragically died when he crashed at 300 miles per hour on this lake in January 1967. The day we visited in 1964, all was peaceful, but it makes me shudder now to think of that accident.

While Chris's compromised eyesight made learning difficult at school, he still enjoyed classes at Northgate Primary School – 'I liked History, English, Art and Music, and to all intents and purposes, I was a good average student' – but his enthusiasm was largely extinguished by the time he reached Hazelwick County Council Secondary Modern School, which was also within walking distance of his home. 'I think the main thing we were taught was to fear authority. The little kids feared the Prefects, the Prefects feared the teachers, and the teachers all feared the board of governors. The masters all wore mortarboard hats and black gowns, and I remember getting caned for ridiculous, inconsequential things, like talking in the school corridors. I think most of the chalkies (teachers) at our school were damaged war veterans, and the atmosphere was plain awful. It was exactly as Roger Waters described years later in his Pink Floyd song *Another Brick In The Wall*.'

The only secondary school activity Chris did enjoy was cross-country running, and it was the only sport he could participate in without being clumsy or teased. 'When I took to the school sports field with a javelin in my hand, everyone scattered as far and as fast as they could. But with running, I found it so invigorating to be outside, and I didn't have to depend on anyone else – I just had to follow the pack. I could keep up with the rest of the runners, so I didn't get razzed about that.'

Being outside complemented Chris's great love of nature. He would often take long walks around his neighbourhood, into Tilgate Park – a part of the Worth Forest, which was abundant with flowers and trees, but without dangerous animals. 'It wasn't as wild as Outback Australia, and I wouldn't exactly find wildlife, but we would catch some newts in the woods.'

The love of animals would become a passion that would define Chris's sister, Susan. As a child, she would be forever taking pity on any wounded creature that she encountered. 'If there was a bird with a broken wing, Sue would be the one to bring it home and gently nurse it back to health,' recalls Chris. Much later, as an adult living in rural Victoria with her husband and two children, Susan would remain devoted to horses and dressage competition. She would also allocate time to provide rides on horses for handicapped children, working in partnership with charities in Victoria.

In contrast to his sister's unwavering love of animals, Chris's great early obsession was with vehicles – all manner of trains, planes and ships. 'I had an avid interest in aircraft, and I just about lived at Gatwick

Airport between the ages of 9 and 13 because I loved looking at all the planes taking off and landing.'

Each September, the Finnen family would travel to Biggin Hill Aerodrome in Kent (a famous RAF fighter station during World War Two) for the annual Battle of Britain remembrance and flying display, which also featured Cold War fighter planes, nuclear bombers and all manner of air transporters. 'There were a lot of aerobatic display teams – The Blue Diamonds, flying Hunters; The Tigers, flying Lightnings; La Patrouille de France, flying Fouga Magisters; and the Yellowjackets (known as the Red Arrows after 1966), flying Folland Gnats.' Chris also remembers the navy displaying Sea Vixens, Scimitars and Buccaneers, many helicopters, and the US Air Force displaying Voodoos, Super Sabres and B66 Destroyers. 'There was a World War Two memorial fly past featuring Spitfires, Hurricanes, Lancaster bombers and Mosquitos, which was greeted with sombre respect by the crowd at the aerodrome.'

In September 1966, Chris remembers being able to attend the Farnborough Air Show. 'It was so great to be there. The weather was marginal, but I didn't care. British aviation was at its peak, with all these wonderful piston-engine, turbo-prop and early jet-engine aircraft – and I got to see them all.'

He would also travel to Gatwick Airport alone, packing his telescope, a thermos of tea and lunch before boarding the 405 Green Line bus to Gatwick, and this occupied just about every weekend and school holiday break. 'We could walk the streets safely and get about as kids, so our parents had no issues. I'm so grateful that it was a much simpler time for a kid to be growing up.'

Chapter 3
A blues record changed everything

There was always music in the Finnen house at Crawley – and it embraced a broad church of sounds and styles. Hawaiian guitar, Nat King Cole, Paraguayan harps, Louis Armstrong, and in particular a swelling orchestral piece called *London Fantasia* that recreated the sounds of The Blitz bombing of London during World War Two, highlighting an aching sadness as bombs dropped and sirens wailed.

Much of Chris's early listening was shaped by what was played on the radio, and curiously his father loved guitar music – even though Jim Finnen had played drums in the Boy's Brigade during his teenage years in Scotland. Jim continued playing drums at lounge room parties on a sporadic basis – mostly using brushes on the drum skins, but sometimes with sticks – but it was the sounds of guitars that caught his ear, especially The Shadows. Chris also recalls hearing Les Paul and Django Reinhardt played on the radiogram at home, which nurtured his early love of the guitar – so much that Chris cut a guitar shape out of cardboard and would mime to the songs.

Chris also became enamoured with the rock'n'roll bands that he would see performing on *Ready Steady Go*, a Friday afternoon TV program that declared 'the weekend starts here' while a parade of bands was filmed performing in the television studio. From this, Chris formed an affinity with both The Beatles and The Rolling Stones, loving the melody and energy of both bands rather than viewing them as rivals. 'Anything good got into my soul. I never suffered from any musical snobbery.'

However, beyond the popular hit parade there were landmark musical discoveries. The most important was receiving a Pye International LP of *The Blues: Volume 2*, from a female school teacher, the year before he left England. This was when Chris first heard Muddy Waters, Howling Wolf, Bo Didley, Little Walter and Chuck Berry. It stopped the 13-year-old boy in his tracks, astounded. 'It changed the way I thought about music, entirely.'

It began a very focused obsession with music, and to learn all that he could, Chris began buying records continuously. This was no act of rebellion in a house that happily hummed to an eclectic musical soundtrack, even though Chris gravitated towards a fair number of raucous songs that his dad didn't approve of.

From the age of 11, Chris would spend all of his pocket money – 2 shillings and sixpence a week – on 45rpm singles and EPs. 'I also used to get 5 shillings a week for school dinner money, so if I went without dinner all week and dug into my pocket money savings, I could get an EP, which cost 10 shillings and sixpence. It was always such a huge decision about what to get. The local record store had a soundproof booth, and they'd play about three songs I'd request and then turf me out, because they figured a kid like me wasn't going to buy anything. After enough sessions of listening to different songs and endless deliberating, I'd finally make the big decision about what record I was going to buy.'

His earliest purchases were an eclectic bunch of hit parade favourites – *Cruel Sea*, an instrumental by Billy J Kramer and the Dakotas; *54321* by Manfred Mann; Johnny Kidd and the Pirates' version of *Shakin' All Over*; The Rolling Stones' *I Wanna Be Your Man* and *Not Fade Away*; the outrageously long-haired quintet The Pretty Things with *Don't Bring Me Down* and *Rosalyn*.

The most important purchase was *The House of the Rising Sun* by The Animals, which became the first song Chris learned to play on guitar and sing all the way through.

He came to many of these songs via clandestine after-dark listening to Radio Luxemburg and the two famed British pirate radio stations, Radio Caroline and Radio London. Over the airways, he'd hear marvellous, exotic sounds that stretched both his musical knowledge and appetite. He particularly remembers being impressed by *My Boy Lollypop*, sung by Jamaica's Millie Small – and this first introduction to Bluebeat formed the beachhead to Chris's interest in reggae that would flourish later.

'I was supposed to be asleep, but I'd have the transistor radio under my pillow with an earpiece. Another big influence was a Saturday morning radio program presented by Brian Matthews called Saturday Club, and any musicians on tour in London would go on that show.'

In time, Chris's music addiction intensified, and he progressed from buying singles to albums – by any means possible. 'My mother gave me some money to buy some new shoes and I came home with LP records instead,' he recalls with a cheeky smile. 'Music became my primary focus. More like an obsession, really.'

The sum of these parts formed the foundation of Chris's early musical education. Because he never learned to read music, he gleaned his knowledge from music captured in the grooved vinyl of his growing record collection and the curious sounds on radio airwaves.

> **I recall the music of 1967 with great fondness. There was so much great music for me to learn from. The Beatles'** *Sgt Pepper's Lonely Hearts Club Band* **was the big one that really revolutionised the long-playing record for me, from the production and the sequencing of the songs right through to the gatefold cover. Jimi Hendrix arriving with** *Are You Experienced* **was equally influential, and there was the great British blues boom, led by John Mayall, Eric Clapton and Peter Green.**

> There were also great things happening in jazz; Roland Kirk, Thelonius Monk, Charlie Mingus, Chick Corea, Miles Davis. And in folk music, I was hearing Martin Carthy, Bert Jansch, Jon Renbourne, Nick Jones and many more.
>
> There was a lot going on – the Monterey Pop Festival led to my discovery of Ravi Shankar and Indian ragas. I heard Frank Zappa for the first time, and the undefinable ideas thrown up by the Bonzo Dog Doo Dah Band and its strikingly eccentric ringleader Viv Stanshall. All this triggered quite a few years of deep, deep study and learning how to play the very best of this music.

His obsessive record buying in Crawley established a pattern that would accelerate once Chris arrived in Australia. He remembers as a teenager that he regarded Melbourne as the Mecca of record shops, and he would haunt the import shops – not only for the discs, but also for UK music papers *The New Musical Express* and *Melody Maker*, to keep him fully informed about new developments within the London music scene.

'I was a semi-permanent fixture at John Robertson's Music in Croydon, and also at Archie and Jughead's and Euphoria Records in Melbourne. I spent all my money on records. It's how I learned about music.'

Among the first albums he bought in Melbourne was local band The Loved Ones' debut album *Magic Box*. A few years later, Chris would get up on stage to jam with singer Gerry Humphreys when he was compere at the Kew Club, a popular dance held in the Kew Town Hall. 'I'd get up with Gerry and the house band to play *Shake Rattle and Roll*. It was a blast.'

However, not every speculative record purchase provided quite what Chris expected. He remembers asking at one record store for an Australian folk album – and was given Chad Morgan's *The Sheik of Scrubby Creek*. 'I thought "What the fuck is this?" The folk music I had heard in the UK all had deep historical roots, and on that first listen, I thought Chad Morgan was just lampooning music. Yes, I was open to weird stuff – I was getting right into Frank Zappa and The Mothers of Invention and The Fugs – but I quicky realised that Chad Morgan was way out on his own. When I finally did start exploring the local folk clubs, I realised they were playing mostly American folk and British folk songs that delved back into very long histories. Recognising Australian culture in folk songs was very narrow at that time.'

Exploring different musical styles in record shops became a type of anthropological fascination for Chris. 'I actually found it really annoying once they started introducing different categories of music in record shops – a separate isolated section for reggae, or for blues, or for jazz. I certainly don't think of music in those terms. Others may find it odd how eclectic my musical taste is, but I feel compelled to chase all good musical ideas.'

It was this appetite for musical adventure that made Chris a favourite customer of the music afficionados who owned Melbourne's most adventurous record shops. Because Chris was forever asking questions, they would play recordings to Chris that they thought he might find interesting. Some fell far outside of conventional music, but he absorbed them all. 'I remember being introduced to a record called *Noises from the Womb* and I found it really interesting because it seemed so familiar. Listening to the pulse of the heartbeat rhythm and the almost drone-like sounds, I heard a really interesting music in that.

'There was also a recording called *Songs of the Humpback Whale* – it came out a decade before whale conservation became a popular environmental movement – and I found it fascinating. It was a soundscape that I realised I could mirror on a guitar, using an echo effects pedal and a slide. I was learning that valuable musical influences could come from anywhere.'

Indeed, Chris's early collection of albums that he purchased after arriving in Australia began to cover very diverse musical terrain, stretching far beyond conventional rock music as he sought to follow the many threads that influenced psychedelia. 'After The Beatles' *Sgt Pepper* album came out, I started looking to India and Africa, to find out more about the origins of the new sounds I was hearing. It also took me further into jazz, and Latin music. The more I heard, the more I wanted to learn.'

Chris's voracious appetite for exciting new music at least helped him win some credibility among his peers at school when he took some of his favourite albums to the lunchtime music listening club at Croydon High School. 'I don't think they quite expected The Beatles' *White Album* and *Magical Mystery Tour* but they sure got excited by what they heard, just as I did. As for Frank Zappa, well, I was out there on my own.'

Chapter 4
Earning the right to play an electric guitar

Chris's obsession with the sound and look of guitars resulted in him being given an acoustic steel-string guitar at the age of 10. His father encouraged him to play the instrument properly rather than just thrash about, and so he stuck numbered labels under the strings as a tactile guide for Chris to learn where each note landed on the fretboard. Jim also bought a metronome to promote strict timing, and a pitch pipe so that Chris could tune the strings. 'I'd learn by playing along to a record – *The 50 Guitars of Tommy Garrett*, which wasn't actually so square as it sounds; it included the song *Maria Elena*, which Ry Cooder later featured on his *Boomer's Story* album.' Even at this tender age, Chris's ears were being tuned to significant music of every flavour, and he embraced it all.

Before long, he wanted to take his guitar out of the lounge room and start entertaining audiences. 'In primary school, I formed a duo with a bongo player called Polly Parrot, and together we played The Beatles' *Twist and Shout* – mainly because I loved John Lennon's scream on the recording.'

Influential 1960s English guitarist Bert Wheedon – who wrote a guitar instruction book called *Play in a Day* (which Chris laments that he never owned) – had a 10-minute segment on television that Chris became fixated with. 'By watching his fingers on the fretboard, I got a clear idea of chord shapes – that the three figures used to form a D chord made a triangle shape.' This became the foundation of Chris's guitar education, giving him a familiarity with aspects of musical notation and theory without ever having formal music lessons. His curiosity led him to learn with precision by ear, so that he could imitate clean sounds on his own guitar with great accuracy.

'Playing along with records was very good for making me get the fingering fast enough and the transition between chords brisk, because the record wasn't going to hang around and wait for you. You had to maintain the tempo, or it would sound like a mess.'

Chris saw the guitar as a means of capturing a complete soundscape. Rather than gravitating to chords as the basis of his guitar playing, he also embraced note-by-note melodies at the same time, forming the basis of melodic solos.

Chris's father also gave him a book titled *5200 Chords*, although he initially stuck to only shaping the major chords. Chris remembers first gravitating to a D shape so that he could wrestle with playing The Byrds' *Mr Tambourine Man*, which was a favourite 45rpm single that he had bought. 'Perhaps the most adventurous I'd been with exploring what was in the book was to play a 7th chord, that one The Beatles had used in the song *Boys*. I haven't even stuck with that chord – I now prefer a 7th with a lower pitch to it – but at least it marked the start of my chord exploration journey. When I did learn a chord that I liked the sound of, I tended to stick it everywhere, like a kid with a new toy. I didn't initially have the patience to learn where the right place for all those chords belonged.

'When I started, all the augmented chords and diminished chords just sounded wrong to me. I thought they sounded out of tune. I kept practising the shapes, so I knew they were right, but I had no idea what to do with these chords. It only came years later, after I'd heard other recordings where there was something fabulous but unusual to the sound that it all clicked for me. The great recordings led me back to those unusual chords.'

The chord book eventually became a springboard for Chris, providing an instruction manual of how to navigate the fretboard, and soon he began to experiment with his own inversions, moving fingers around from standard chord shapes to chase more interesting tones that pleased his ear.

While pulling apart the chords as he played, Chris began to ponder how sounds are made, and built an understanding of what notes work best together. Without realising it, he began to appreciate the formal structure of music.

'My ears started to open out in a new way. I began understanding the recordings I listened to in a different way. I came to realise that the melody at the heart of The Beatles' *Twist and Shout* was the same as *La Bamba*. Trini Lopez had a hit in England with *If I Had a Hammer*, and it was the same chords again. I began to hear all the connections within music, and that understanding chords and notes on the guitar fretboard would unlock them all.'

Playing the guitar soon became an important aspect of Chris's identity. 'Because of my bad eyes, I wasn't running with the other kids and I didn't really fit in. I couldn't play sport because my vision made me so clumsy, and I wasn't at all interested in the military cadet corps at school, but having a guitar really brought me out of my shell. It never made me over-confident – just very happy.'

However, being a cavalier 13-year-old guitarist still got young Chris in trouble for being a bit too risqué, playing a bawdy folk song about infidelity called *The Manchester Molecatcher*. 'I didn't understand the sexual inuendo. I just heard the tune and liked it, so I played it at a Cumbrian youth hostel when our school went to Scotland on holiday – and the lady who ran the hostel picked me up, carried me to the kitchen sink, put a bar of soap into my mouth and hung me up by a clothes peg stuck to my duffle coat hood. She said: "A young man like you shouldn't be singing words like that!" I had a lot of apologising to do, and it was only then that I actually learned that the song was about a married woman having sex with another man while her husband was at work.'

While his acoustic guitar served as the fundamental training tool that schooled Chris in chord shapes and fretboard fingering, he was always pushing to get an electric guitar, so that he could start making sounds like the bands whose recordings and performances on TV were propelling his excitement in music.

Chris finally got the electric guitar that he craved after the Finnen family had arrived in Australia and settled at the Nunawading Migrant Hostel. A Futurama guitar, complete with tremolo arm (a model of guitar that George Harrison also used), was a gift for his birthday on Christmas Eve that had been secretly packed by his parents when they departed England, and while he adored the guitar, he had no amplifier. It didn't matter to Chris. He immediately set about furiously shaping the chords, working his hands on the fretboard and finding that his fingers could move fast along the slender guitar neck, which enabled him to play more notes more quickly than on an acoustic guitar. It provided the inspiration for him to devote even more time to practising.

Obtaining that first electric guitar changed Chris – even though he didn't realise it at the time. His English Aunt Mary, who had travelled with the Finnens to Australia aboard the *Ellinis*, watched the transformation from close range. It wasn't until she was 87 that Aunt Mary told Chris that his electric guitar gave him a sense of confidence that he'd never had before.

'Once I was in Australia, the guitar became very important to me. I just didn't fit in with other kids, but I became important in some of their eyes by default through being able to play the guitar. It opened up opportunities for me.'

It also became his sole obsession. 'My interest in planes and all other forms of aircraft took a back seat. I'd taken the tram from my home to Essendon Airport a few times, but I never found it as interesting as Gatwick Airport, because there wasn't the same bustle of international planes coming and going. I kept seeing the same types of light aircraft again and again, so aviation became a sideline interest and music dominated my every waking moment.'

Before long, Chris stepped up to a better model of electric guitar – a 1965 Egmond Typhoon (made in Holland, Model 034-3V), with three chrome pick-ups and a vinyl-covered body. 'I still have one of these lovely guitars, thanks to the help of my friend and fellow guitarist Gary Allen, who tracked it down.'

As every guitarist knows, just having one guitar is never enough. But it was a desire that baffled Chris's mother. 'When I bought a second guitar, she asked me "Why do you need two?" and thought I was being rather excessive.'

Over the years, Chris's collection of rare and beautiful guitars has, at times, extended to beyond 50 instruments. 'I collect guitars for the joy of playing them. They are truly beautiful. You caress them, and they allow you to communicate with your fellow human beings.'

While he continued to learn more about music, Chris didn't take an academic approach. His poor eyesight provided a stumbling block that thwarted easy progress with musical theory and writing notation – but his hearing became especially acute to compensate for poor eyesight, and this enabled Chris to quickly recognise and process musical passages through careful listening. Painstaking rehearsal in the company of his record collection and stereo speakers became Chris's passport to improvement on the guitar.

'I didn't give up on things that didn't work – not even when this occurred much later during performances. It just meant that I'd have to go back to practise them again and again in private. There's always more work to do.'

This included learning how to bend notes on the guitar fretboard, which Chris had heard so effectively on classic blues recordings. He couldn't get access to light-gauge guitar strings, and his 15-year-old fingers struggled greatly with trying to bend thick strings – so he got the tip to use thinner banjo strings instead and tuned them differently to get the right sound. By doing this, he could bend notes a full tone with these more flexible strings. It set him on a regime of practising the bending of strings to achieve perfect tone, along with curling his little finger around the guitar's volume knob to create a weepy sound that he'd heard on his favourite records – sounding just like the guitar effects pedals that he couldn't afford.

'In the era when I learned how to play the guitar, you just had to remember things. There was no online resource showing you step-by-step tutorials on how to play your favourite song. You had to reflect on the performances you'd heard in a venue and the records you listened to – and often your recollection wasn't perfect, so the music you made would just come out your own way.

'People say to me that I'm lucky to be so talented, but to be honest, talent didn't just drop out of the sky and hit me. I had to work very hard to train my ears, and it came through practising every day. I still do, which is how I've developed my own individual voice as a guitar player.

'To progress, I had to improvise, compromise and rationalise. I didn't have all the equipment these guys had in the recording studio. I never had a really good guitar until I was 21, which was a cream-coloured Fender Telecaster, with a bridge pick-up that could cut through concrete.

'I made it my mission to get the best sounds out of what I had – and that took a lot of trial and error, endless rehearsing and listening carefully to everything I was doing.

'I've always listened to music in an analytical way. I've listened to so many different players and I would concentrate on their tone, their phrasing, and my sound therefore has its history formed from all of the many things I've heard. I never consciously chased my own thing with playing the guitar, it just emerged over time. And suddenly, it appears – your own signature.'

Guitar wasn't the only instrument that fired Chris's imagination. His father's interest in playing drums rubbed off on his son, and Chris would pound out a beat to his favourite records with anything that came to hand in the family home. After a period of Chris furiously hitting cushions in the lounge room with sticks, Chris's father came home from work one day and produced a paper bag containing a pair of wire brushes, which inspired Chris to experiment with sounds created by a lighter percussive touch. He'd turn over the lounge room pouffe stool and tap out rhythms on its wooden base, playing along to his dad's LP records of jazz and Latin music. 'They were the only LP records in the house. I only had singles and EPs, so I'd put Dad's albums on because they lasted for much longer – and this developed my deep love of jazz and Latin rhythms.'

Curiously, Chris's hunger to learn about guitar was motivated by his collection of 45rpm pop and rock singles, yet his rhythmic delights came from LP jazz records, with these two seminal yet separate musical influences seeming to exist in parallel universes. 'I suppose I was listening to those jazz records with a different set of ears, deliberately searching for the percussion focus. Listening and tapping along to Dave Brubeck's *Take 5* and *Unsquare Dance* – these were lightbulb moments for me. The rhythms were so exciting and I now understand that I was listening to the whole musical package. It wasn't just one instrument that caught my attention. I was listening to a whole band, and this informed my ideas about how to make music. It taught me some big fundamentals, that good timing is so important – and yet I was terrible at maths in school. It was my worst subject, but I understood very complex time signatures implicitly. If there was long division on a blackboard, forget it, but in a musical format I could cope with complex rhythmic patterns quite well.'

Earning the right to play an electric guitar

Having enjoyed the simple delights of whacking brushes against an upturned pouffe, Chris soon wanted to experience more percussion – although he was more interested in hand percussion rather than attacking drums with sticks, as it was primarily the intricate types of rhythm patterns that gabbed his attention. 'I remember being enroute to Australia in 1967, when the ship docked at Aden, and my mother bought a double-skinned drum for me from a local market. I loved mucking around with the high and low tones of the different sized skins to create these beautiful rhythm patterns – but once we docked in Australia, that animal-skin drum got confiscated by customs. I lost the drum, but not the affection for how it sounded.'

It started a lifelong love of percussion that persists to this day, with the front room in Chris's Seaford Rise home featuring an incredible menagerie of drums from different cultures around the world – djembe, congas, tabla, darbuka, timbales, doumbek, along with a conventional drum kit and cymbals. Given the slightest prompting, Chris starts tapping out rhythms, usually exotic and often complex, on whatever is close at hand. 'The rhythm is in me. Guitars aren't the only instrument I can use to release the music that's inside of me.'

With an array of instrumental tools at his disposal to create music through his early teenage years, and with the dedication to diligently rehearse, Chris was quickly building a bridge between his love of listening to music from the record collection he was amassing and the desire to create music for himself.

All he needed was the opportunity to get up on stage and play.

Chapter 5
All-night gigs in Melbourne

The first music clubs in the heart of Melbourne that Chris attended to experience live music at the end of the 1960s were The Thumpin' Tum, Berties and The Catcher. These were gigs that ran all night long – but he was only 15 years old when he first entered them, having taken the train into the city from Mooroolbark in the outer suburbs. 'There were bands playing everywhere in the city – and I would go to three venues a night. It would start on a Thursday night, because Thursday was pay day for the vast majority of workers, and the gigs would go all Friday night and Saturday night. I wanted to stay until the last band came on stage at 1am, determined not to miss anything that was happening, so I'd usually miss the last train that travelled back out to the suburbs. I'd walk around town all night after the gig, until I could get the first train back home the next morning – but it was worth it to see that final band of the night.'

Watching bands on stage became Chris's formal education in musicianship and performing. 'When bands performed on stage, all the songs would be stretched out longer than the recordings, with all these incredible solos added in. Some of the most wondrous things I heard on stage never made it onto a record. I felt like I absolutely had to be there to experience those rare moments.'

Inspiration and musical enlightenment came in many forms. Chris remembers David Hubbard, vocalist with the Captain Matchbox Whoopee Band, coming to Croydon High School to give a performance and workshop during a music lesson. 'It got me into jug band music, which also came into the local folk clubs around that time as well. I heard washboard and tea chest bass for the first time, but I also heard these great jazzy melodies – and I came to understand that the jug band movement was another connection to jazz. It got me learning a whole lot of different chords that I would not have seen until much later. If I didn't learn those tricky chords, I couldn't play the songs – and that's the thing about jug band music. It's not so simplistic. There's more in it than what meets the eye. So much music is like that.'

Absorbed by his own ad-hoc musical education, Chris decided to leave school when he was 15 and announced to his parents that he would dedicate himself to music. 'I didn't plan music as a career move. It's just something I did because I was compelled to. I remember my stoic Dad always saying to me "When are you going to get a real job?". He wasn't very impressed by my decision.'

Chris had tried to get regular jobs, but his limited eyesight presented significant problems in trying to obtain permanent employment. He had already endured five operations on his good eye in a thwarted effort to improve visual clarity, and Chris had also suffered vitreous haemorrhaging (bleeds from ruptured vessels in the retina) that would temporarily rob his eyesight for indeterminate periods.

Amid all this, he took a job in a lumber yard, to earn much-needed cash. It was a disaster. 'My poor vision made me rather clumsy, and one day I tripped, which bought down a huge pile of timber on top of me, and I got a knock on the eye which made things even worse. Needless to say, that job didn't last.'

Because Chris's eyesight was so poor, when he attended gigs, he would always stand immediately in front of the stage, enabling him to check out everything the musicians were doing. They soon became very familiar with the skinny bespectacled kid peering at them, full of enthusiasm and firing off endless questions. 'They were so friendly, which encouraged me to always ask them more and more questions about everything they were playing, and their answers kept feeding my interest.'

Through his constant questioning, Chris learned a lot of secrets about technique. It was a time of experimentation, and he showed great discipline as he devoted himself to learning the nuances of his instrument – along with trying to figure out how the master guitarists achieved their distinctive sounds. For instance, how did Eric Clapton achieve that fabulous tone in *Badge*? 'After endless mucking around, I found that what Clapton calls his "woman tone" on the guitar required me taking all the treble off the tone control. In trying to solve some of these mysteries, I was often looking for a complicated answer, yet in the end I found it could be so simple.'

Soon, an eager Chris was jumping up to join acts on stage for impromptu cameo performances. He especially remembers having a jam with Billy Thorpe and the Aztecs on New Year's Day 1970 at The Thumpin' Tum. 'It was the first time I'd played through such a big amplifier – and it nearly blew my ears off. It was so exciting. When those guys allowed me onto the stage, all of my dreams about being a musician became possible. Their generosity and encouragement helped my talent to flourish.

'I was just so excited at being invited to fit in that it really overrode any anxiety I had. Sure, I was nervous about getting on stage, but once I started playing, it always felt pretty good – so I thought that the wonderful exhilaration of performing was something worth being nervous for. In fact, I've always found a that a degree of nervousness is useful, because it stops you from being blasé about performing for an audience.'

While he was getting familiar with what it felt like to play guitar on stage, the access that Chris obtained to a host of experienced musicians who invited him to jam also provided valuable guidance. 'I must have been an absolute pest because I was always asking questions, but they gave me great answers that provided the clues I needed to keep progressing as a guitarist. Their generosity taught me a creed that sticks with me to this day, that I will always help another musician if they ask me a question.'

Chris especially remembers generous guidance he received from Reno, a Maori ex-pat in Melbourne who played guitar in the band Compulsion. Reno took the time to teach Chris a repertoire of Jimi Hendrix licks – and they stuck. 'Hendrix was one of my big inspirations, but I never tried to copy him note for note. I wanted to play my own interpretation of Jimi, not copy him.'

While his intensive guitar education was in motion, Chris had also started playing in his first band – St James Infirmary, which performed its first gig in 1968 at the Dorset Gardens Hotel in Croydon. Other shows were at Boronia Town Hall, The Piccadilly in Ringwood, and Sgt Peppers in Box Hill. The early set lists featured songs by Cream, Jimi Hendrix, Traffic, John Mayall and the early Fleetwood Mac – songs that Chris and his bandmates had eagerly acquired from import record shops and were all brand new to the ears of Melbourne audiences. 'I was only 15, by far the youngest one in the band, and I looked up to them all. They sacked the singer, and they made me sing while I also played guitar. They later joked that they bullied me into it, because none of the others in the band wanted to sing.

'I'm eternally grateful to the help given to me by my friends and bandmates Wayne Viney, Bob Molk, Andrew Staples and Bill Magill that made playing in St James Infirmary such a life-changing experience. Even though I was so naïve, it gave me the incentive and confidence to try pursuing a career in music.'

Rehearsing with the band formed only a part of Chris's development as a guitarist. He would also hire a hall in the neighbouring suburb of Kilsyth, between 1pm and 5pm each Saturday, and also hire a Marshall amplifier. He would assemble any musicians who were interested in having unstructured jam sessions, and would take along a portable cassette recorder to capture everything on tape that unfolded. He called it 'freeforming', and he would spend the following week poring over the cassette recordings, listening carefully to everything during the jam that worked – and also take note of what didn't gel. 'That's how I learned to identify the flourishes that were good,' says Chris, 'and the bits that weren't so good, which were the parts that I had to keep rehearsing, to make them better next time.'

He was learning quickly, and was starting to feel vindicated by his decision to quit school in favour of devoting all his time to playing music. However, not everyone shared his enthusiasm. Chris laments that his gruff Scottish dad only came to see his son play about four gigs. At one, Chris was feeling pretty cocky and confident and was showing off on stage, tipping into unnecessary excess. Afterwards, his father said tersely, 'People are paying good money to come and see you play, so they deserve to see you at your very best'. Chris says the criticism stung him, mainly because he realised the ring of truth in what his father had said. He'd placed hollow showmanship ahead of his craft, and he vowed not to repeat the mistake. 'He saw straight through my nonsense – and that has always stuck with me. Even if you're trying your heart out to entertain people, you don't abandon your craft.'

The initial plunge that Chris took into the live music scene of Melbourne – both as an eager observer in the audience, and as a nascent performer – formed an important part of a very busy musical education, which also combined with his exploration of many different musical styles and sounds. Chris was acutely listening to learn, through playing a mix of gigs in electric rock and blues bands while also performing solo acoustic gigs in coffee houses to play traditional folk music. 'I used to love doing those folk gigs, because that was the big opportunity for me to sing while I played. I was adding something to my musical knowledge every single time I performed, and I never saw anything wrong with doing everything all at once. After all, I had all this music inside of me. One way or another, everything had to come out.'

This was an era when a lot of paid gigs occurred each week, both in Melbourne (at such venues as The Thumping Tum, Bertie's, Lucifer's and Catchers) and through a scattering of suburban Town Hall dances – at Boronia, Kilsyth, Sgt Pepper's in Box Hill, Impulse in Prahran, Stonehenge in Beaumaris, Piccadilly in Ringwood, White Elephant at Broadmeadows, and The Kew Club.

'The Town Hall gigs had three bands performing, so each band did only one set – which meant you could do more than one gig on a night. We'd play up to five gigs a week, mostly from Thursday to Saturday nights. There would be a few other engagements in between. We played at a clothing boutique in Melbourne called The In Shop, setting up our equipment among the racks of clothes while people shopped.'

Chris would also supplement his earnings from electric gigs with acoustic folk gigs in coffee shops. 'That was easy for me, because I could just take my acoustic guitar on the train to get around. With all of my electric gear, I'd need somebody to provide transport for me and the equipment because I couldn't drive.'

The sum of these performances was enough to pull together a moderate wage, which enabled Chris to leave home at the age of 17 and live with other musicians and friends in a series of flats and share houses. It also enabled him to buy his favourite all-time guitar in 1969 – a vintage Fender Jazzmaster. 'I played this guitar so much. I used this for many studio recordings, and for all my touring right through the 1980s with the Matt Taylor Band, and I really regret selling it – but to be honest, I'd completely worn it out by that stage.'

It was a formative time for Chris, as his band St James Infirmary remained busy as a gigging band until 1971. The bandmates formed strong friendships, and Chris remains in touch with drummer Wayne Viney and bass player Bob Molk (keyboard player Peter Luke also played in the band for a while). It all helped to forge a musical vision that would shape Chris's musical direction for at least the next decade, built around the furious blues/rock power trio foundation laid down by Cream and the Jimi Hendrix Experience. 'I've got a set list that this band played in 1968, and a lot of those songs – *Stone Free, Crossroads, Money Honey, Sunshine of Your Love, Hey Joe* – are still part of the repertoire that I'm playing today.'

The band changed its name to Concrete Wellington – 'That was my idea of a wordplay piss-take on Led Zeppelin' – but the membership disbanded, Chris moved to Box Hill and formed a new outfit built around a similar set of musical ideas, and also called the new band Concrete Wellington. Significantly, that band formed only part of Chris's musical focus, as he also spent a lot of time sitting in with Doug Parkinson In Focus, Chain, Billy Thorpe & The Aztecs, Langford & Leaver and Ross Hannaford. He also remembers that Lobby Loyde provided many useful tips on guitar playing, especially how to use a plectrum. 'I spent a lot of time just hanging around and listening to lots of other bands – and I became really close friends with Phil Manning and Ross Hannaford. I fondly recall this time as my essential apprenticeship.'

Phil Manning remembers Chris coming to his home in South Caulfield for many jam sessions. 'It was a happy hippie vibe and there was great camaraderie among the young musicians,' says Phil. 'It was such an exciting time because there was so much innovation happening with sounds and recording, and we were all so keen to see what everyone else in our scene was doing.

'We were all on this same journey of discovery in music, and Chris and I both liked the same guitar players – Freddie King, Albert Collins, Robert Johnson – but his appreciation was much broader, and that reflects in Chris's style of playing the guitar.

'We'd all sit around together and listen to the important new albums as soon as they were released. I remember Lobby Loyde bursting through the door with a copy of Fresh Cream by Cream, and we just kept playing it over and over. This big gathering of guitarists was just so fascinated by the sounds that our instruments were making.'

However, Chris had many struggles outside of learning his musical craft. His vision had become very erratic, which led him to have the first of several guide dogs – as much to serve as a safety measure as a sight aide. 'It was in 1972, and I got beaten up while travelling on a train by a punch-drunk ex-boxer. He bent my metal cane and started laying into me. Nobody on the train did anything. Later, a girl I knew who was the kennel-master for the guide dog school heard about the beating, and recommended a dog for me, mainly to ensure my safety.'

Phil Manning remembers Chris's guide dog fondly. 'I can remember going with Chris to a concert at Festival Hall in Melbourne – I'm pretty sure it was John McLaughlin and the Mahavishnu Orchestra – and I was marvelling that his guide dog remained so calm throughout the gig when there was this tremendous noise going on all night,' says Phil. 'I suppose this was something that really bonded my friendship with Chris. I had very serious eye issues when I was a child growing up in Davenport, Tasmania, and if it wasn't for the intervention of a doctor, I probably would have lost my eyesight during primary school. I understood what it was like to endure vision problems, even though I suffered nothing like the difficulties Chris faced.'

Chris admits it wasn't easy to persevere with his vision difficulties without making a fuss. 'It was a period when my vision was especially volatile and kept fluctuating. It really rattled my confidence, so the dog was a really important companion and provided crucial assistance to me for a while. But once the vision in my left eye stabilised again, things became easier.

'However, I really loved the dog a great deal and was very grateful for its help and companionship. I've always been a lover of dogs. I say that life without a dog is incomplete.'

Chapter 6
Commencing a love affair with Adelaide

In June 1974, Mary and Jane Birmingham – who had been playing some traditional English and Celtic folk music with Chris at folk clubs in Melbourne – both shifted to Adelaide, to do a course at Flinders University. They invited Chris to come over from Melbourne to perform some gigs during their mid-semester break, but his intended one-week vacation in Adelaide marked a big turning point in his life.

The trio played gigs at The Catacombs on the corner of North Tce and Dequetteville Tce, and at the Mile End Hotel, which had become a haven for Adelaide's folk performers – and the environment felt just right to Chris. He was listening to a lot of Fairport Convention and Steeleye Span at the time and his big record collection proved to be a valuable source of material for the Birmingham sisters. Indeed, a song they found within Chris's collection – a Scottish border ballad called *The Border Widow's Lament* – was later recorded by Mary after she moved to Europe, and her rendition achieved acclaim among European folk circles.

Chris initially stayed at the Birmingham sisters' house in Glenelg. During that first week in Adelaide, he met Fred Wachtell, who had a flat at 234 South Road, Mile End – which was owned by Bruce and

Ros Hogben (Bruce was a journalist at Adelaide's morning broadsheet newspaper, *The Advertiser*). 'I remember sitting around, smoking a few joints and listening to *HMS Donovan*, having a truly lovely time, and Fred said he was going over to Ballarat to court a girl he had met. He asked if I could stay for a few weeks to look after his flat, so I did – and I made a few friends quickly, played some more acoustic folk gigs at a coffee shop in Glenelg, and really started to settle into the place. Fred came back and announced "I've fallen in love with Ruth, so I want to go back to Ballarat", to which I said "I've fallen in love with Adelaide". I took over the flat in October 1974, and my life in Adelaide took root.'

It soon became a place Chris was happy to call home. He began playing regular folk gigs at The Catacombs, the Mile End Hotel, The Saint Coffee Lounge in Glenelg, Ginger's in Melbourne St, North Adelaide, and at the Traitor's Gate Folk Club in the Earl of Leicester Hotel at Parkside, although Chris's rather liberal view of how to present folk music ultimately saw him come into conflict with some folk purists who organised the gigs. 'At one point, I liked the idea of playing these songs on an eclectic guitar, so I took along my favourite Jazzmaster guitar to the Traitor's Gate Folk Club and was setting up a Fender amplifier – but several disgruntled people stood up and left the gig before I'd even started playing.'

At this time, Chris was also playing in a jug band called Slapdash, with vocalist Isobel Storey, Bob Petchell on guitar and clarinet, a tea chest bass player and Chris on acoustic guitar.

Chris was simultaneously doing electric gigs, having formed the first incarnation of The Chris Finnen Offering in 1976. This first version of Offering, with Tony Lewis on drums and Michael Hodson on bass, was especially busy, scoring regular high-profile gigs for Patrick O'Grady's Bijou Shows and Peter Dawson's Sunstone Shows that were held at suburban town halls, along with gigs in the various university taverns and refectories. It gave Chris enough work and enough musical diversity to be satisfied with his decision to remain based in Adelaide.

Finnenisms

Sometimes you feel many miles away. Sometimes you cry for help.
You stood alone and no-one came, except perhaps another self...
In rooms of voices, darkness calls. There's no-one else around.
Just you afraid and all alone as you crumble to the ground.

Miles Away, by Chris Finnen, 1976

While the original Offering trio parted company after about a year, with the other players wanting to do other musical projects, a second version of the power trio soon formed, with Mick Ridge on bass and Paul Turner on drums. This outfit became a fixture of the Lone Star suburban pub circuit, playing regular gigs at the Broadway Hotel in Glenelg South, the Seacliff Hotel, the Marryatville Hotel (including a rather bizarre double billing with seminal Australian punk band Radio Birdman), The Largs Pier, The Tivoli and the Kent Town Hotel.

Their blooming popularity saw Chris Finnen Offering invited to appear on *Rockturnal*, ABC TV's progressive rock program which was hosted in its first season by Dave Woodall. Recorded in late 1977 but broadcast nationally on May 31, 1978 (with Ayres Rock, Charles Mingus, Stiletto featuring Jane Clifton and Garland Jeffreys also featured on the same program), the *Rockturnal* experience saw the band get paid $30 for its efforts.

It was at this time Chris met Karen O'Sullivan – 'an absolutely wonderful human being' – during a gig he performed at the Tivoli Hotel. 'We got talking afterward, and I got her phone number. I didn't have a phone at home, so I had to go down the street to a phone booth to get back in touch with her, but I made sure that I did, because I thought she was really special. We hit it off immediately.'

Within a year, they were married. Chris remembers that they were both very considerate of each other, even when their marriage broke down after seven years. 'She was a career woman, working as an executive secretary, and I was away touring a lot of the time, and we just grew apart. We never stopped loving each other, but our lives were going in different directions, and we both realised that it made more sense for us to pursue our individual journeys.'

Although he felt settled in Adelaide, Chris remained restless as a musician. Taking yet another left-turn, he sat in as a semi-permanent member of country-rock band Redeye. 'They needed someone to cover a guitarist who had left, and the Chris Finnen Offering played on the same circuit of gigs, so I joined Redeye at the Seacliff Hotel every Wednesday and Saturday night, while also carrying on with my own band.'

Another popular residency was The Broadway Hotel at Glenelg South, which was part of Ray Dyett's Lone Star circuit of venues. A large crowd would come to hear Chris Finnen play on alternate weeks to hard-edged blues band Mickey Finn, whose bass player Bruce Howe and their sound engineer Frank Lang later hooked up with Chris at a backyard party in Glenelg. Frank informed Chris that he also played bass guitar, which laid the foundation of a long-lasting musical partnership that first gelled on stage with Chris Finnen and Friends. This comprised former Fraternity members Mick Jurd on guitar and John Freeman on drums (they had also formed the band Some Dream) with Lang on bass, playing gigs at the Windmill Hotel on Main North Road in Prospect (famed for featuring The Sensational Bodgies as its resident attraction). Frank remembers Chris launching into lengthy solos trying to imitate whale songs, only to have Jurd respond comically on his Les Paul guitar with loud mooing noises. Still, there were also some great chordal improvisations played by Finnen and Jurd, taking the music deep into the realm of experimentation.

Chris led another short-lived venture in 1979 called Band of Hope, an ensemble built around two drummers driving the rhythm section, along with bass player Mark Smith. 'It was basically the same Finnen repertoire, but with this mighty sound of two drummers at work. We had Dave Gorham on a powerful rock kit and Kieran playing a lighter jazz kit. We largely put it together for fun, so it only lasted for about six months before the various players drifted away to other ventures.'

Chris's reputation as a guitar firebrand also had him hosting guitar workshops, and one memorable guitar clinic at Regent Music in Adelaide featured an appearance by the esteemed British amplifier builder Jim Marshall. This was the man whose Marshall Amplifiers were made famous by Jimi Hendrix, but Chris knew Jim was originally a jazz drummer, and had instructed Mitch Mitchell, who later became drummer in The Jimi Hendrix Experience. 'While we were doing the clinic, I asked Jim if he'd like to get on the drums and join us for a song or two. He was rather shy, but his wife was with him and prompted him to get up and play. He had this huge smile on his face, and afterwards his wife told me that it was the first time he'd played the drums in many years.'

Chris also became a regular fixture at Derringer's Music, teaching guitar to students in the rehearsal studios and forming a strong friendship with owner Peter Vitek, leading to late night jam sessions in the shop ('I remember Peter playing a beautiful red Gibson 335 guitar through a small Ampeg amplifier turned up really loud – and he sounded great!') and more than a few guitar purchases from Derringer's over the years.

While all this musical activity was happening, Chris's flat on South Road quickly became a drop-in centre for all manner of Adelaide musicians, and it was also where Chris began teaching guitar to an eclectic array of students, both young and old.

'When I'm teaching, my main goal is to help a player to find their own voice – and the easiest way to do this is to lead by example. I try to make people feel comfortable with the instrument, but I also have to underline that the instrument will not play itself. You must work at your craft.

'My methods must work, because I've bumped into students 40 years later who have kept the lesson tapes we made together. That makes me so happy. I may not know as much as the world's great virtuoso musicians, but at least the things I pass on have stuck with the people I've taught.'

He fondly remembers teaching Tim Parker, a gifted journalist who worked at Adelaide's metropolitan afternoon newspaper *The News* and Channel 9. He was also a mainstay bass guitarist of many popular Adelaide pub rock bands (including The Blue Meanies, Flash Harry, No Tiser Required, The Dags and X-Pats). Tragically, Tim died from cancer in 1995, aged only 38, and Chris performed at a memorial concert for Tim held at Thebarton Theatre on December 9, 1995, with proceeds donated to cancer charities.

Chris is also especially proud of having mentored two masterful, multi-talented and hard-working musicians in Josh Bennett and Paddy Montgomery. 'One of my great thrills has been to present a budding musician on stage for the first time. While I have passed them the baton, they have, in turn, passed it back to me. I've learned just as much from them in return.'

Over the years, Chris Finnen Offering became a vehicle for Chris to explore many musical ideas, and moved far beyond conventional rock music to embrace the prog influence of King Crimson, especially as a third incarnation of the Offering took shape from 1979, with Peter Nixon on bass, Dave Pike on drums and Neil Kowald on keyboards. 'I was a bit under the spell of guitarist Robert Fripp and I wrote a song called *Lack of Oxygen*, which had some really strange time signatures (previous versions of Offering had tackled a prototype version of this song, called *Triangles*). I wasn't adept enough to play like Robert Fripp or John McLaughlin of the Mahavishnu Orchestra, but I'd hint at it. I was crazy and ambitious, but I still knew what my limitations were.'

This final version of Offering, which performed until 1981, began to work across a broader stylistic range, incorporating more reggae, psychedelia and a hint of blues into the repertoire.

Then a call came from Matt Taylor, the leader of seminal Australian blues band Chain. Chris had remained good friends with everyone in Chain from their years together in Melbourne and jammed with them whenever they passed through Adelaide. When guitarist Phil Manning announced that he was leaving the band, Taylor rang from his home in Perth, asking Chris to try out for his new band. 'I travelled to Perth during 1981 for a trial and that worked out fine, forming the foundation of the Matt Taylor Band. As a result, I rented a house in Perth, but I was married to Karen, who still had work in Adelaide. After my role in the Matt Taylor Band was formalised, Karen came over to join me in Perth a few months later. It was awkward though, because the Matt Taylor Band would go out on three-month tours that went around Australia – and for a while I'd be living out of a suitcase in hotel rooms while still paying rent for two residences in two cities that I wasn't living in.'

Blues now became the sole focus of what Chris was playing. 'I was so aware that what I had to play for this band was the guitar parts laid down by my great friend and guitar influence, Phil Manning,' recalls Chris. 'I approached his body of work with the greatest care and respect.' He also started co-writing songs with Matt and their compositions formed the basis of the album *Always Land On Your Feet*, which blues fans rate among Taylor's best work.

Being in the Matt Taylor Band also represented a new set of musical constraints placed on Chris, who played a specified role within the group under Taylor's leadership, which was very different to him exercising complete freedom as a solo artist. 'It worked well, and Matt and I became quite close,' remembers Chris, 'both as friends and musical accomplices. I found this a very exhilarating and enjoyable experience.'

The friendship extended to Matt taking extra care with looking after Chris on the road, as he was travelling with a guide dog for much of the Matt Taylor Band's touring regime. 'We'd try to fly rather than drive to a lot of the gigs – and that got us into a lot of first-class lounges once they saw Chris's guide dog and then offered us assistance,' says Matt. 'I loved that dog, but I couldn't spend any time in the same room with it before something horrible happened. It would sit on my glasses and crush them, or fall asleep in the middle of my hotel bed before I'd even had a chance to put my bags down.'

By the end of 1984, Chris's stint with the Matt Taylor Band had come to an end. 'I think he just wanted to play more of his own music, because there's no scope for people to do their own material in my band, but he left with my blessing,' explains Matt. However, Chris surprised everyone by heading in an unexpected direction. He decided to travel with his wife Karen to Melbourne – and embark on a very different chapter in his life. He quit playing music as a full-time occupation and took a job as public relations officer for Seeing Eye Dogs Australia. 'Because I had a seeing eye dog for a while, the organisation approached me to be the public figure who could do presentations on its behalf at schools and service clubs. It was an educative role, and a really refreshing change of pace for me.

'I wouldn't say I was burned out from touring with the Matt Taylor Band, but I just thought that the job with Seeing Eye Dogs Australia would be really interesting and that I'd be able to really help people. That aspect appealed to me greatly, but after a year in that role, I just missed music so much that I had to quit the job. I'd actually kept my hand in by playing on weekends in a cabaret band, just being someone anonymous who played guitar in the background, but it wasn't very satisfying. I was in limbo. At this point, I realised that my true calling was music.'

By early 1985, many aspects of life in Melbourne were not working for Chris. His marriage to Karen had broken down, and his passion for his job with guide dogs had stalled, so he decided to return to Adelaide. 'While I realised that I could live anywhere, as long as I had music and a roof over my head, I knew that I had a lot of friends in Adelaide – and it was the only place that I actually missed when I wasn't there. I came back into town by train from Melbourne and just seeing the landscape pass by my window, I realised my heart was here in South Australia. It was a very emotional realisation. It should have been obvious to me but I had to go away to really feel that this city is where I want to be.'

Chris rented a ramshackle little flat in the city's west end, opposite Adelaide's historic mosque in Little Gilbert St, and he immediately set about playing music with lots of different sets of friends – and he appropriately called this loose performing outfit Chris Finnen and Friends, specifically so he could perform with whoever was available to play. The band name also served to underline that he wouldn't be tied to work with any specific set of musicians.

'I didn't develop any set plan to re-establish myself in the Adelaide music scene. I was just eager to get out and play all the time. This loose performance collective provided the opportunity for me to address all the musical ideas that had been stored up in my head. It was the exact opposite of the defined structure that I'd been sticking to for three years in the Matt Taylor Band.'

It was an especially busy time, with Chris playing a hectic mix of band performances, along with solo gigs that required him to play three sets a night on acoustic guitar and sing. He now admits this 'was physically very demanding, but boy, I learned a lot about how to entertain audiences when it was just me making all the music. It demands something of you to engage with a crowd and keep their attention for an entire night. It really made me hone my skills.'

He even formed a short-lived cover band with bass player Frank Lang, called Slab, a light-hearted venture playing a motley collection of rock favourites at venues including The Marion Hotel.

Chris also did regular duo gigs with bass player Peter Howell, who was travelling from Melbourne. Ultimately the strength of their relationship led to Chris and Peter forming a trio called National Collection with drummer Robin Andrews, and which only ever performed in Victoria and Tasmania. Peter also played with the great Melbourne-based blues singer/songwriter/guitarist Dutch Tilders, which led to Chris forming a strong friendship and long-lasting musical partnership with Dutch.

> **I had known about Dutch for a long time, and once we met, we formed a deep friendship. There was so much music we**

played together, on tour and at festivals throughout Victoria, South Australia, New South Wales and Tasmania. His well-seasoned voice and expertly-crafted guitar playing was such a pleasure to enjoy, as was his company. He was a very well-read, intelligent man, and there were many unknown sides to him. For example, he was a great stride and boogie-woogie piano player, but so few people ever got to hear him do that. I know this because he just started playing for my son Izaac one day, on an old wooden upright piano in our house.

I'll never forget the final time I got to play with Dutch in public, after he had contracted cancer and so many musicians and friends came together for his Cancer Benefit Concert at Thornbury Theatre in Melbourne on 29 July 2010. It featured the cream of Australia's blues fraternity. I'll never forget borrowing a guitar from Phil Manning, and joining Phil, Matt Taylor, Dutch and many others at the end of the gig, for what would be the last time we played music together. It was a very emotional experience for all of us, and Dutch literally gave every last drop of energy, soul and commitment that he possessed in that final peformance.

I must make mention of Lynne 'Peanuts' Wright, who did so much for Dutch and worked so hard to put together such an important milestone in Australian blues history.

Dutch sadly passed away from cancer on 23 April 2011, and his funeral and wake were attended by just about every blues and folk musician who could get there. My son Izaac was with me and I was glad he was there, because we both miss Dutch so much. Izaac's favourite memory of Dutch was him sitting with Izaac and me in our backyard at home on a hot summer's day, all of us with our shirts off, devouring a large bowl of yabbies. Simple, happy days. I'll be forever grateful that I was a friend and got to play so much music with Dutch Tilders.

These expansive friendships and musical opportunities in different parts of Australia occurred due to the sum of Chris's incessant guitar playing and gigging through almost three decades. 'Because I'd built up a national reputation through the Matt Taylor Band, it had become more credible for people from different cities to agree to play with Chris Finnen. Even though I was interested in a lot of different music, I was happy to be known mainly as a blues guitarist – but it never stopped me from doing all the other music. Focusing on the blues material actually helped me understand my different and specific roles. It resulted in a lot of opportunities that led to touring around Australia with many different outfits.'

The late-1980s also became a period when many people tried to start marketing Chris – with one suggesting he play up the 'blind boy bluesman' angle that mirrored the handle adopted by many of the pioneer American bluesmen, including Blind Boy Fuller, Blind Lemon Jefferson, Blind Willie McTell and Blind Blake. This notion gained further traction after the late-1990s international success enjoyed by gospel harmony group Blind Boys of Alabama. But it was an idea that deeply irritated Chris, who wanted no further attention drawn to his sight impediments. 'There were plenty of people critical of me who had no interest in understanding the extent of my condition, so I felt it more important to inform only my friends about the vision problems I was going through, and I believed it would be counter-productive to make it public knowledge.'

Fellow guitarist Phil Manning, who suffered his own serious vision problems during his childhood, believes Chris's vision difficulties may have heightened his other senses, and subsequently influenced his intuitive style of improvisation on the guitar. 'Perhaps his compensation for poor eyesight is a heightened appreciation of tone and more acute attention to hearing sounds,' says Phil, 'because with Chris, both of those attributes are very distinctive.'

Chris, however, has always played down such links. 'I saw the "blind bluesman" image as being a really cheap gimmick, that had nothing to do with my music. I also felt it could really be a big distraction to what I do as an artist and that my vision problems could end up dominating any conversation about me, so I wanted nothing to do with promoting such a notion.'

It underlined the fact that Chris maintains a very open-ended philosophy about what he wants to do in his musical life. He has long realised that pursuing such an eclectic path was always likely to be at odds with the sorts of plans and schedules that a manager would want to instil. It has led some people to declare, in exasperated tones, that Chris was 'unmanageable'.

'People kept telling me that if I had a manager, I could have gone a lot further with my music career, but it never worked out that way for me. You see, I never thought of myself as just a blues player. I want to make a lot more different types of music, because that is what I listen to and where I get fresh ideas. It is also what I enjoy, and that simple love of music is essential for me to hold onto. I play the music that I want other people to hear.'

Throughout this era, Chris seemed to be playing with just about every notable musician in Adelaide on a regular basis, dispensing with the era's accepted code that players stayed true to only one band. By contrast, Chris thought very differently about how he should share his talents around, and as a consequence he now recalls this period as an intensive phase of his learning.

Beyond frequently changing musical collaborations, a change of dwelling was also necessary in 1991, after the ceiling collapsed on top of Chris as he laid in bed in his Little Gilbert St flat. 'It was a fiercely hot day, and I was lying in bed because I couldn't see. I'd had another optical haemorrhage during a period of pronounced visibility problems, before corrective surgery stabilised what was left of my limited vision. And the next thing I knew, I was covered in chunks of plaster and had no idea what was going on. I didn't have the phone connected at that house. Thank God someone happened to pop over to say hello. I was in a right mess.'

He moved house to Windsor Gardens, thanks to help from the Housing Trust of SA, and then his life took another significant turn as romance bloomed from a chance encounter at a gig. Chris met Dawn Edgington during a Sunday afternoon blues barbecue at the Earl of Leicester Hotel at Parkside, a casual jam session organised by harmonica player and energetic gig promoter Greg Baker. After a whirlwind romance, Chris and Dawn were married. It lasted five years. 'We were both rather free spirits, and we had a wonderful time together but, ultimately, we went our separate ways. There was never any sourness between us, and we still talk – she lives in Perth – but our lives were heading in different directions, and we both recognised that.'

Chris's schedule became a busy clutter of gigs. He sat in with rockin' blues band The Others during their weekly residency on Wednesday nights at Lennie's Tavern in Glenelg, and band leader Ian Nancarrow asked Chris to join as a permanent member during 1985. 'I always thought of working with that band as just a part of the many things I was doing, but playing with The Others had priority ahead of other gigs,' explains Chris.

A car accident enroute to a gig in Port Pirie put the band in temporary recess during 1986, when Ian and Chris played a run of gigs as The Others Trio, with Peit Collins on drums (a regular in Greg Baker's Blues Party, who later relocated to Melbourne and won national attention with recording trio The Sharp). This fledgling trio was fortunate that Ian's friend Greg Petty, a former champion superbike rider, had a light plane and was keen to clock up extra flying hours in the pilot's seat, so he would fly the trio and their equipment to gigs throughout rural South Australia. 'It was the only way we were going to get to well-paid gigs at Whyalla,' remembers Ian. 'After the car accident, Chris was understandably reluctant to be in a car for long trips.'

Within a year, however, the band folded. 'At some point, Ian got upset that I was sitting in and jamming with several people around town,' recalls Chris. 'He informed me that The Others didn't play outside of the band – to which I replied that I do jam with other people. It was uncomfortable for Ian, but I wasn't going to change.'

One of these regular sit-ins was a Saturday night graveyard shift at The KoKlub in Hindley St (a room that later operated, until 2023, as Enigma Nightclub), playing from 1am until 5am with Gary Allen (from The Healers) and bass player Michael Winter, who would eventually become a member of the Chris Finnen Band. Chris was such a fan of these all-night jams that he would take along a packed lunch box, to keep him sustained with sandwiches and snacks through the marathon sessions. 'It never bothered me to be playing all night and again the next day. I was just having a great time being at the centre of a very active scene, and I was still buying heaps of records and listening to lots of influences. You could say my music studying period was happening in earnest at this stage.'

Having left The Others to pursue a broader musical spectrum, Chris would also sit in with The Healers, and with the earliest incarnation of bass player Frank Lang's blues band Hoy Hoy! in 1988, with former Mickey Finn drummer Joff Bateman. In time, Hoy Hoy! – which was steered by Frank through an epic 27-year journey – would come to feature drummer Trapper (Trevor Draper), who before long would also play a very significant role in Chris's future musical endeavours.

Chris began playing Sunday afternoon blues gigs at The Oriental Hotel in Norwood with a nascent model of The Chris Finnen Band and guests, including cameo appearances by his friends Dutch Tilders and Phil Manning whenever they passed through Adelaide.

Beyond all this, Chris's fascination with Indian music took full flight as he launched into a pair of inventive experimentation projects, thanks to an unlikely connection made by music promoter Peter Dawson. 'He used to come to my flat all the time and listen to music with me, so Peter knew about the full scope of my musical interests. He became the connector that introduced me to Krishna Kumar and Professor Michael Junius, which led to the Indian/jazz fusion ensemble Indian

Pacific – and through performing with that group, I was approached by Dya Singh to play guitar for his Sikh music ensemble. I said yes to every opportunity because I wanted to learn.'

As the spread of musical styles in the Finnen repertoire continued to diversify, so the exotic influences began to inform other areas of Chris' music. 'By the late 1990s, I suppose the Indian scales and tones had seeped into my musical subconscious without me realising it. I remember an American traveller coming to several gigs I did in Adelaide and telling me after a blues show that he loved the Indian influence that he heard in my solos. I thought he was getting confused with the Indian Pacific gig I'd played the previous night, but then I realised that I was beginning to fuse the different threads of musical influence in my mind, and it was coming out in how I expressed my solos. I was on a path to truly creating my own sound.'

Chris also got involved with many Adelaide performance organisations during the 1990s – including vision impaired advocate Tony Doyle's Arts in Action concerts, and the annual South Australian Folk Festivals held in Victor Harbor and later in Goolwa. Chris also worked with Dave McPharlane (now sadly deceased), who taught migrants to read and write English at the Blair Athol Language Centre. 'He'd take all his young adult students to the markets on an excursion, and then they would bring all the food back to the college for a cook-up while I provided some music. I'd explain the songs and they would have conversations with me in English. It was a really great learning environment for them.'

Chris would frequently volunteer to play music in old people's nursing homes, and in schools. 'I could see that music was helping many kids at school. Music wasn't being taken as seriously as sport in schools. I knew what music had done for me, so if I could encourage any kids to take music onboard, it could provide them with a lot of happiness, and perhaps a new set of opportunities.'

It marked a significant moment of reflection in Chris's life, and a realisation that he had something of value that he could give back

Ready for another day at Northgate Primary School.

Chris with his sister Susan and mother Elizabeth on the border of Scotland and England, 1960.

At the formal dinner table aboard the Ellenis, with (from left) Uncle Bob, Fleur (another migrant passenger), Jim "Jock" Finnen and Elizabeth Finnen, Chris, Roland Idris Lloyd and Aunty Mary, January 1967.

Chris at work on his first electric guitar – a Futurama, complete with tremolo arm (a model of guitar that George Harrison also used) – with his sister Susan at the Nunawading Migrant Hostel, Melbourne, February 1967.

15-year-old Chris with St James Infirmary, on stage at the Dorset Gardens Hotel battle of the bands, 1968.

St James Infirmary rehearsing in drummer Wayne Viney's lounge room, Melbourne, November 1968.

Rehearsing in Melbourne, 1968, aged 16.

Chris Finnen Offering performing at the Broadway Hotel, circa 1977.

Chris rehearsing in his Windsor Gardens flat, circa 1992.

Jeff Lang (on mandolin) with Chris (on electric guitar) and Phil Manning (on acoustic guitar), on stage at the Lewisham Hotel, Sydney, 1980s.

Chris playing his beloved red Fender Jazzmaster guitar, with his matching glasses, hat and t-shirt clashing violently with entirely inappropriate trousers, at one of Greg Baker's Hahndorf Blues Festivals, early 1990s.

Chris on acoustic guitar with Indian Pacific in the 1990s, featuring Professor Michael Junius (on trumpet) and Krishna Kumar (on tabla).

Chris with Matt Taylor, playing a Chain gig at Clarendon Hotel (photo by Samra Teague).

Performing with Colin Offord, in Paddington, Sydney, early 2000s.

On stage at Kay Brother Wines with the Chris Finnen Band, 2020 (photo by Samra Teague).

Chris with Dutch Tilders and Matt Taylor on harmonica, at Dutch's Cancer Benefit Concert, Thornbury Theatre, Melbourne, 29 July 2010 (photo by Rooster McBlurter).

Taking his music into the crowd at a Barossa music festival, early 1990s.

The patron of the Port Noarlunga Blues Festival, playing at a festival fundraising gig in 2019 (photo Samra Teague).

On stage at WOMADelaide with the Chris Finnen Band, 2012.

Scat vocals and bottleneck acoustic blues, on the porch at Fox Creek Winery cellar door, McLaren Vale.

One of the most colourful of Chris' vast collection of guitars and ethnic stringed instruments from many different cultures.

Chris surrounded by his acoustic instruments during a gig to promote his 1997 album *360 Degrees*.

Chris's shiny steel Dobro guitar always draws attention from audiences.

Author David Sly interviews Chris on stage during the 2023 Adelaide International Guitar Festival (photo by Milton Wordly).

Chris performing at the 2014 Adelaide International Guitar Festival, hamming it up with bass player Frank Lang (photo by Tony Lewis).

Never afraid of adopting a unique look, Chris has experimented will all manner of stage personas – from a dyed red afro in the mid-1970s, to leprechaun sideburns in the early 2000s, to outlandish colour-explosion jackets that remain a Finnen signature to this day.

to the community. 'I see music as being fundamental in reinforcing a larger sense of community. Because of my vision problems, I know that I don't fit into the standard picture of what society expects, and yet I still have something powerful to contribute. So, I've jumped at any opportunity to use the language of music to bring people together. If I got offered payment I'd take it, but I didn't need payment to get involved in something I thought was worthwhile – just as long as someone could get me to the gig and get me back home afterwards.'

Chris notes with pride that musicians are always the first to volunteer when a benefit is organised to help someone in crisis. 'Using the power of music to help our fellow human beings is a no-brainer. It always works. Some of the reasons for staging these events can break your heart, but at the end of a benefit concert, a lot of people go home happier, having been nurtured by the power of so much love in the room.

'A colleague once told me that I do too many benefit concerts, but the truth is that you can never do too many. If you're still breathing and can play, you have a duty to help.'

There's a lot of me you never see. I've got feelings deep inside.
Just try to live my life somewhere in between my fortune and my pride.
Sometimes when I go to sleep at night, I get funny visions just behind my eyes.
There's a whole lot of love left inside of me.
I just want to give a slice to you.

Feelings, by Chris Finnen, 1978

His willingness to contribute has taken Chris to many unusual places. A fan who came regularly to gigs was also a hospital orderly, and asked Chris to play guitar for teenagers who were having dialysis treatment. 'They were hanging around in this big common room, playing pool and chatting, generally just doing their own thing, and I'd brought along an acoustic guitar and was wondering what the hell I should do. It wasn't as if they were waiting for me or even expected me to perform. I was just some old fart with a guitar who had wandered in. I started playing a bit of blues, and by the end, all of them were listening. They were tough nuts to crack – I had no idea whether they liked it or not – but the orderly wanted me to come back a few months later, so this time I brought an electric guitar and an amp, and I walked into a very solemn room because one of this group of teenagers had died recently. I took it gentle and played an Indian raga for about 30 minutes – and I found out later the deceased teenager's parents were in the next room and said that the music helped them in their grieving. That moment was important. You often never know the effect you'll have on different people through what you do. For me, it reaffirmed what the power of music can achieve.'

Chris says every volunteer gig he's done has provided a special memory that he holds on to. 'I cherish a photograph taken of a child at the Woodville Spastic Centre, probably about 1980, who was reaching out to touch me while I played the guitar, with a look of delight on his face, and I had the same joy written all over my face. It looked like we had both been given a million dollars. That's what music can do for you.

'I feel a moral responsibility to share music with people who may not otherwise have an opportunity to go and experience it – so I bring it to them.'

> **Music should be accessible to everyone, and if they can't get to you, then you have to present it to them. Performing in retirement homes is a very good example of how to do this. I remember playing a concert at a nursing home in Victoria, which included a community sing-along of songs from my parents' era, like** *When You're Smiling* **and** *When the Red Robin Goes Bob Bob Bobbing Along.* **A lovely old lady using a walking frame had a melodica with her (a hand-held keyboard driven by blowing into a mouthpiece) and she began to play along with me, although she was cutting many of the musical phrases in half, or kept adding a few extra bars to the verses – but she**

was holding court and everyone at the home loved her. So, I changed my guitar accompaniment to fit in with her musical world, and it was great.

At another nursing home concert, I encountered a dapper, immaculately dressed but rather fragile old Welshman, who was sitting next to his daughter (and she was older than me). I decided to honour him by playing an old Welsh hymn, *All Through the Night (Ar Hyd Y Nos)*, which captures a true essence of the Welsh spirit. As I played this tune, he began whistling along with great power and vibrato. His daughter informed me that he hadn't done that in many years – proving that music opens doors within people.

I was once made aware of an old Romanian lady who was bedridden and couldn't attend a concert that I had planned at a retirement home, so I told the organisers that I'd like to go to her room and give her a private performance. She was so excited that she had been awake with anticipation since 5.30am. She told me she had played the violin when she was young – but even though she had been in this home a long while, nobody else knew about this. It's amazing the conversations and shared confidences that musicians have with audiences.

I visited Kangaroo Island with Slava Gregorian and friends to perform as part of the Adelaide Guitar Festival, which included a lunch-time variety concert at a nursing home in Kingscote. While Slava was setting up the sound system, I noticed a group of old folks gathered around a table, singing old-time songs as one lady was strumming on a ukulele. I wandered over, sat down and took out my acoustic guitar and joined in. It was such fun – a beautiful spontaneous moment that I'll never forget.

Chapter 7
The ever-changing, long-enduring Chris Finnen Band

The emergence of the Chris Finnen Band as a blues power trio during the 1990s gave Chris a more solid shape to his performing regime – and it occurred because he found a set of musicians who could best read his instincts and travel with his ideas. The group also brought a more specific blues focus to his performances, drawing a circle around his strengths as an instrumentalist and for being distinctly different through his World Music explorations.

While Chris continued doing solo gigs – and folk performances, and journeys into World Music, and experimental music ventures, and sitting in as a guest with all manner of performers – the Chris Finnen Band became the cornerstone of his musical identity, being able to stretch in many directions yet still hold together and remain strong as a musical unit.

One of the essential members of this band has been drummer Trapper (Trevor Draper), who first came to play with Chris 30 years ago, arriving as a package deal rhythm section with Frank Lang from Hoy Hoy! when the 1990s-era Chris Finnen Band first took shape.

'It was like all the players from different blues-based bands were inter-woven,' says Trapper. 'I first started playing with Chris when he called on me to do fill-in gigs, and in time, I became the drummer he would always be calling on. Over three decades, the musicians who have played regularly with Chris became like a big inter-connected family.'

Trapper's rock-solid downbeat emphasised the blues-based core of this electric band's personality. 'Trapper says he's a rock drummer who I got to start playing swing,' says Chris. 'He has tightened up the sound of my band a great deal, but the music still has a looseness and freedom about it. He gives me the best of both worlds.'

Trapper is similarly complementary of Chris's musical guidance, which he says has expanded his style of drumming. 'Chris is rarely given credit for his knowledge and ability as a percussionist,' says Trapper. 'He has turned me on to Indian percussion, African percussion – things I never would have been exposed to if it wasn't for Chris and his eclectic music tastes. He has this incredible appetite for complex polyrhythms, and when he starts explaining his rhythmic ideas for a particular piece of music, we both read each other instinctively. That's why we've worked together so well on stage for so many years; I've learned to read all his signals, so that I know where he's going to take the music once he starts improvising. In those moments, it's such a thrill to hang on for the wild ride.'

The other mainstay of the electric ensemble has been bass player Michael Winter, who first started making music with Chris while he was just out of his teenage years, as a jazz student at the University of Adelaide. He was a band colleague of guitarist Gary Allen in The Healers (which had previously been called The Blues Healers), and this partnership led to Michael becoming a fixture of late-night jam sessions at KoKlub in Hindley St, Adelaide, from about 1987. Chris became a central figure in this informal jamming group, and he also became a mentor for both the young musicians. Michael says he was surprised but also greatly energised by Chris's enthusiasm for encouraging young musicians. 'It was overwhelming at times, because Chris is such an incredibly gifted and extroverted lead guitarist, and it felt like I was just clinging on by my fingernails when we played music together, but he became this extraordinary guide who led me down so many exciting musical paths.'

Chris included Michael in a short-lived trio – Los Trios Bentos, with Mick Garcia on drums – that experimented with different styles of blues, and while Michael says he learned a lot from playing live with Chris, he believes he has picked up more musical ideas through hanging out at Chris's home and exploring his extraordinary record collection. 'He had a better jazz record collection and knowledge of jazz music than some of the lecturers I had at university,' says Michael.

It was here that Michael learned about some of the great jazz fusion bass players – such as Darryl Jones (cohort of Miles Davis, Sting's *Dream of the Blue Turtles* band, and now part of The Rolling Stones) and Ray Brown (famed for his work with Oscar Peterson and Ella Fitzgerald). 'Listening to these guys taught me there is no such thing as just a standard way of playing blues,' says Michael. 'There are the alternate chords, along with substituting jazz chords to make passing runs more angular than the standard blues progressions. Listening to these guys showed me there are great rewards that come from trying to push the envelope.'

Just as Chris had done during his own formative years of learning about music, Michael began to implement the many ideas he gleaned from listening to records – and because he sourced these inspirations from Chris's record library, it meant that they both shared a shorthand understanding of how various musical ideas could be joined together. 'In time, Chris and I developed a connection on another level. I know where he is going to go with the music before he launches; it's instinctive, and it's a feeling that we can both read in each other at all times. It means there are no restrictions to what we are doing when we are working as a trio. We have the capacity to just fly. But as soon as someone else comes in to join us, adding another voice to the music, the restrictions come back in and I don't feel that we can just instinctively push the musical boundaries so much.'

Such willingness to improvise is the attribute of Michael's playing that Chris most admires – and it puts Michael in the rare position of being able to push Chris into unexpected musical territory during songs, rather than Chris always being the leader.

'Michael has a much larger musical vocabulary than most of the other bass players I know, because he has a very good feel for jazz and Latin grooves – and he plays both electric bass guitar and double bass,' explains Chris. 'That gives me the confidence to take my music further. He throws musical ideas at me that I have to follow, and I really like that challenge.

'That's why I'm lucky to have this band. They are very good musicians who understand me, and to my ears we make such very enjoyable music. They are always listening, always have their radar on. I consider them the best rhythm section I've ever had, because they allow me to diversify.'

However, it took time for this intuitive spark to ignite, and the Chris Finnen Band's foundations and early journey was laid down by a different cast of characters. By 1994, the Chris Finnen Band had developed a reputation as a formidable live performance entity, featuring John Freeman on drums, who was famous for his work with legendary Adelaide rock bands Fraternity, Mickey Finn, and then in the first incarnation of Jimmy Barnes' solo recording and touring band. John came to work with Chris after the demise of The Flyers, a hard-working blues outfit that featured guitarist Dave Small, harmonica player Dave Blight (also noted for being a Cold Chisel sideman, having played the haunting harp solo on the famous song *Khe Sanh*) and bass guitarist Frank Lang – who would eventually be called on to make the leap to join Chris Finnen Band.

The initial role of bass guitarist was taken by Michael Winter, who Chris was keen on performing with regularly. 'It was the ultimate musical education for me,' says Michael. 'Not only was I playing with Chris, but also with John Freeman, who is a master of time. He was teaching me the essential rhythmic foundations of every aspect of blues, and then there was Chris teaching me all the harmonic extensions of what its possible in blues. The two of them taught me the best of all worlds at once.'

John's wife at the time, Sue Freeman (now Suzanne Jarvis), took the role of band manager. She was involved with the SA Blues Society, and could see great potential for the band on a national level, but realised that a more focused work commitment was required, so set about forming stronger connections within the music industry.

This line-up recorded a live album at the Governor Hindmarsh Hotel, and the *Chris Finnen Blues Band* CD was released by specialist blues label Exile Records in 1994 (owned by the national Festival Records company), a label which also featured Adelaide expatriate guitarist Mal Eastick (formerly of Stars).

Some strong reviews of the CD that were published in national newspapers and the music press led to a solid regime of touring, but the serious question of whether or not to move interstate and take on a much heavier performance workload led to a serious fracture in the group. Michael Winter had finished his teaching degree and earned a posting to Mount Gambier; he wanted a guarantee that Chris Finnen Band would be able to pay him a wage comparable to his new teaching job. No such guarantee could be ensured. And Chris was unwilling to move from Adelaide and sacrifice his Housing Trust-subsidised dwelling; he wanted short-term tours that would lead him home to Adelaide.

'I felt that if the band didn't become more visible interstate and make strong connections where the big bosses in the music industry were located, then it wouldn't be able to progress to the next level,' remembers Sue Freeman. 'And when they all couldn't agree on whether or not to relocate, that's when things stalled.'

Michael went to teach in Mount Gambier, and wouldn't reconnect to perform with Chris for another five years. Dirk DuBois joined for a while on bass. He had previously performed with Chris as part of

Chain, but after a few months of very enjoyable music and friendship, Dirk moved on to Brisbane. It formed an important connection; Chris would often fly to visit Dirk and join him for a series of trio gigs in Queensland, and in Brisbane they would often have the good fortune to be joined by Kirk Lorange (famed session slide guitarist and noted for his work with Richard Clapton) for Sunday evening sessions at the Healer nightclub in Fortitude Valley.

Next to the group came Frank Lang, from Hoy Hoy!, who had done stints as bass player in many Finnen ensembles since the late 1970s – but the initial momentum that the Chris Finnen Band created had been fractured, and wouldn't heal. John and Sue Freeman grew unhappy at what they saw as a lost opportunity.

Despite frustrations regarding the ambitions of the band, they at least enjoyed some truly memorable gigs tied into idyllic fishing excursions on the far west coast of Eyre Peninsula. 'I remember going to Venus Bay and no-one was around, so we'd go fishing,' recalls Sue Freeman, 'and then the empty pub would start to fill up once the sun went down, attracting all these farmers and fisherman from hundreds of kilometres away – and a really wild night was had by all.'

In time, John Freeman left the band, and by 2007 the Chris Finnen Band changed shape yet again, with Trapper taking over the drum seat, Michael Winter coming back to Adelaide and taking on bass guitar duties, and the sound taking a tougher, more direct and hard-hitting approach.

The thread that remained consistent throughout this journey was Chris's playlists that combined his original material with classic standards and cover versions. 'At every gig, I would always play a percentage of my own original songs but also my interpretations of other people's songs that mean something to me. I'm never interested in just playing a cover version – going note-for-note to imitate the original version – because I always want that beautiful song to breathe new life. I know this has resulted in people from the audience saying "we quite often hear you play the same songs, but never the same way", and I like that, because it signals that they recognise there are sections in these songs for creative improvisation.'

As the Chris Finnen Band continued to work in fits and spurts through the next few decades, Chris always maintained strong ties with the core members. This happened even when Chris came to issue a solo album in 1998 with The Crossing Record Company – an independent label created by music-loving Barossa winemaker Rick Burge – because he still found space to include his band colleagues on several tracks.

This solo album certainly embraced the essential blues core of Chris's music, being significantly different from two other Finnen albums that Rick funded and released through The Crossing Record Company – the acoustic duo album *Finnen & Lang: Live at the Vineyard* (with Geelong-born guitarist Jeff Lang), released in 1996, and the very diverse World Music collection *360 Degrees*, released in 1997.

While blues was central to Chris's solo album, it embraced a very diverse tapestry of styles. Called *From the Kitchen Table . . . to the Bottom of the Morning*, the album comprised a wily mix of 16 original Finnen compositions, and it represented many of Chris's various performing guises – from virtuoso solo guitarist on searing instrumental tracks, to his duo work with Melbourne bass player Peter Howell, and introducing another studio band featuring American-born bluesman Mike Festa on pedal steel guitar. It also features Trapper and Frank Lang laying down a tough backbeat on the raucous *Boa Constrictor* and *Keep Your Oven Warm* – two tracks that would be reprised by the Chris Finnen Band for its 2021 album *To My Southern Town*.

The solo album struck a note with blues fans around Australia, winning three awards at the Goulburn Blues Festival, but sales were slow. It marked the end of Chris and Rick Burge's partnership. 'The Crossing Record Company needed a commercial success, but it didn't happen,' says Rick. 'It added a lot of strain to what we were doing, and it all just ran out of puff in the end.'

Reaching a crossroads at this juncture led to a bigger question of where the sum of all this musical activity was headed – and what was the intended destination for Chris Finnen. In Chris's mind, it was always about remaining eclectic and expressing all of the musical ideas that come to him, which includes mixing his original compositions with other people's songs, but never playing them note-for-note like the original recordings. He knows this isn't the key to commercial success, but he's comfortable that it sits within his definition of artistic integrity.

The lack of sales success with recordings hasn't spelled an end to the Chris Finnen Band, though. 'This outfit is incredibly durable,' says Trapper. 'It's built as much on friendship as it is musical chemistry.' It has also led to other opportunities, as Chris's links with Trapper and Michael Winter have resulted in all three being recruited by Matt Taylor (and also bass guitarist Frank Lang) for sporadic gigs as the Adelaide incarnation of Chain. 'It's important for me to work with these guys, because they help keep the legacy of Chain alive – and Chain is the main vehicle where we can express an Australian take on the blues,' says Matt. 'They're all great players, and Chain demands that, because we've never played straight 12-bar blues. It's all about the subtle signals and changes all through the arrangements. So, I'm lucky; I've got an Adelaide version of Chain, and a Sydney version of Chain, and I've got guys like Chris and Trapper and others who understand it all and bring this very Australian flavour of blues to life every time we take it to the stage.'

Despite Chris's keen appetite for live performances, he was never keen to remain out on the road for long periods. The permanence of Chris's Adelaide roots drilled down deeper when he moved south to Seaford Rise in 1999. He had applied to the South Australian Housing Trust to transfer from his existing rental property at Windsor Gardens (about 12km north-east of Adelaide's CBD) to a new house at Seaford Rise (about 35km south of Adelaide). It was located near his partner at the time, who had become pregnant – and Chris moved into his current residence during the year that his son Izaac was born. 'I just had to be near him, and I was lucky enough that this house became available. Now, it's the longest I have lived anywhere.'

The move to the far southern suburbs wasn't an easy transition, as Chris's inability to drive a car always leaves him dependent on other people to transport him and his equipment to gigs. Suddenly, being an extra distance from the centre of Adelaide meant that his availability to perform some gigs became more fraught. Chris wasn't fussed; he considered his relationship with his infant son to be of much greater importance.

'Izaac moved in with me at Seaford Rise by the age of three, so both of us are very attached to this place. Izaac grew up here and went to school here, so his friends are here. He's a skateboarder and there are great skate parks here, so it made very clear and simple sense to stay here rather than go back into town.'

The house has seen a parade of famous musicians coming through the door for regular visits, and Izaac grew up being showered with affection by the likes of 'Uncle' Matt Taylor, 'Uncle' Phil Manning and 'Uncle' Dutch Tilders. 'Everyone that he knew was a musician. Izaac therefore thought that everyone played music.'

The Chris Finnen Band played on, and the introduction of Ian Jeffrey on congas, bongos and all manner of hand percussion came in early 2000. He adds some of the percussive flourishes that Chris is so fond of playing himself when jamming at home with his imposing arsenal of percussion instruments from around the world. 'Ian provides the sounds that I'm already hearing in my head,' explains Chris. 'People were confused when I asked Ian to join the band, wondering why I didn't add another guitarist or a keyboard player, but I believe percussion adds lovely colour to the music without crowding the space.'

Ian, who is originally from Sydney and moved to Adelaide in 1990, learned percussion from Keith Casey (from seminal Australian jazz-rock band Ayers Rock) and he played in the Sally King Band before shifting cities and taking residence in Seaford Rise, only a few streets away from where Chris lives. The seeds of their firm friendship – which has seen Ian provide enormous help to Chris by driving him to many gigs – began when Ian was playing percussion in the Mike Festa Band, which hosted casual weekend jam sessions in the late-1990s at The Roundhouse, a beach-side venue in Moana. Soon, Chris was hanging out at Ian's house for Friday night margaritas and enjoying fun-filled impromptu jam sessions. Then Chris sat in during gigs with Ian's longstanding duo CWilly, alongside guitarist Gavin Truscott. Having enjoyed these gigs, Chris involved Ian in more jam sessions with his own band colleagues, and when CWilly finally dissolved, Chris asked Ian to join the Chris Finnen Band.

'Some percussionists just don't understand what belongs in a song and they are so over-enthusiastic that they fill every space, all the time. Ian's not like that,' explains Chris. 'He's understated. He instinctively understands what a song needs, and understands when to be minimal, or even to not play at all. In tastefully adding the right flourishes at the right time, he brings a wonderful warmth and versatility to our music. I really couldn't imagine the band without him.'

In its current form, Chris Finnen Band has produced two significant milestones that catalogue the great strengths of the ensemble. *To My Southern Town* is an album of original blues songs recorded in 2021, but is far from a straightforward affair. The master guitarist takes his band through a procession of different blues styles – stomping boogies, brisk shuffles, bouncing 12-bar progressions, screaming blues-rock skyrockets – yet through it all a common thread prevails, of Chris's sublime guitar providing compelling blues signatures to savour.

Like all of Chris's recorded compendiums, it's a journey that meanders – from the spooky, swampy weave of *Giving Up The Church*, to pyrotechnic solos on the aching slow blues *Forty Four Years*, the rock-hard drive of *To My Southern Town* and the slippery swing of *South Australian Outback Blues*, interspaced by the charming wobbly gait of the jaunty instrumental *Lilli's Strut*. There are two heartfelt gems that dazzle – the poignant reflection on mortality *All My Friends Are Going Down That Lonesome Road*, and the soaring, Jimi Hendrix-infused opus *Feelings*.

As always, the songs convey exactly what Chris is thinking – often delivered with such open and naïve honesty that sentiments may seem corny (such as the endless food puns laced through *Keep Your Oven Warm*) or blithely conversational (such as his luddite grizzle on *Don't Send Me No Email*), yet the heartfelt delivery of these songs is never contrived. After all, this is Chris's personal blues, told through the prism of a suburban Adelaide perspective and not a cookie-cutter homage to Americana. It shines specifically because of that honesty.

Chris Finnen Band also issued *Live in Lockdown 2020*, a DVD that accurately captures the energy and vitality of a Chris Finnen Band performance, which is like trying to catch lightning in a bottle. Just committing the sounds to audio files seems to miss the essential excitement of what happens in the moment, and so the decision to film a single performance in the Global Music Revolution video studio has provided all the essential visual cues that demonstrate just how this four-piece band clicks together as a cohesive unit on stage.

Sure, the focus is largely on Chris's fingers, as he flays them all across the fretboard while assaulting a wide array of guitars, but we also see his band cohorts Trapper, Michael Winter and Ian Jeffery revving the engine that propels this performance with verve and muscle.

The 11 tracks featured on this DVD chart a big course through Chris's diverse career, embracing so many different musical flavours and cultures. There's a significant nod to his early Jimi Hendrix fixation (with *Stone Free* and *Little Wing*), but more important is the delicious jaunty dance of Abdullah Ibrahim's *African Marketplace*, and a poetic interpretation of Pachelbel's *Canon in D*.

Of course, there's also the essential blues foundation stones – namely the soaring bottleneck howl of *Weepin' Spell*, his original slow blues opus *Forty Four Years* and racy shuffle *PMT*. Through all this, it's

Chris's extraordinary command of the guitar – wrenching, bending and conjuring notes from every part of his instruments in ways that often beggar belief – that keeps the viewer transfixed.

For everyone involved in this enduring ensemble, it hasn't been an easy journey to travel the distance with the Chris Finnen Band. There are opportunities that have slipped away, and other possibilities that never eventuated. However, there is a calm understanding among the personnel that this is Chris's band, and things will always be done in a way that Chris feels most comfortable with. 'We are there to provide the platform for Chris to do what he does at his absolute best,' says Michael Winter. 'I play in many other outfits as well, so I'm happy that this is entirely Chris's vehicle for doing what he wants, in the way he wants to do it. It's his name that sells the band, and his reputation that brings the audience, so Trapper and I are there to bring it all to life. Every time we come together, we very easily resume the musical conversation, right from where we left it last time. Chris really seems to appreciate that we will always be there to provide a bedrock to his music.'

The release of the new album and the process of recording a DVD during COVID-19 lockdown has even given the band a fresh lease of life. Due to this, Michael is confident that Chris Finnen Band still has a distance to travel.

'We are well aware of the jibes – that the set list doesn't change, that Chris doesn't write enough new material. One woman described us as the band that plays the same song all night. But I think Chris has earned the right to have honed a set containing all his best work. All the great bluesmen have created their show, and they play it every night – but mostly in a different city every other night. People in Adelaide get to see Chris perform all the time, so they become very familiar with what he does – but I can bet they never see the same performance twice.'

Chapter 8
Open to all influences

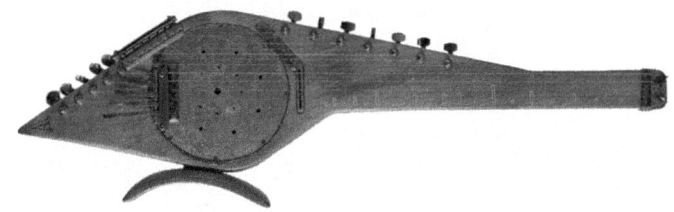

Chris Finnen needs to express himself through music. He explains it as a physical need, but also a spiritual connection and a vital social interaction with others. The complexity of such dynamic expression encompasses much more than blues – and for Chris it always has. He says all the music of the world adds up to the sum of his being. It explains why he performs, and why his performances are so eclectic, including so many musical styles and cultures. 'My voice sings for my heart,' he explains. 'My guitar sings for my soul.'

This becomes apparent whenever Chris tries to explain the essence of his musical inspirations and passions. Words are never quite adequate, never able to fully illustrate his thoughts, and when he starts fumbling to find the right words, he instinctively reaches for a guitar and starts playing a tune to illustrate what he means. Once he has a guitar in his hands, it all becomes very clear – and the music flows out of him, effortlessly, as it travels to every point of the musical compass.

Perhaps the most understated yet profound influence at the core of Chris' musicality is jazz. This was his father's first choice in music, and while Jim Finnen preferred a rather straightlaced style of jazz that carried an easy swing and sweet vocal melodies, his record collection provided a pathway for Chris to continue exploring the jazz idiom.

Open to all influences

'I could understand jazz because I recognised the blues roots at the foundation of it,' says Chris. 'I came to love jazz because it was so different – the virtuosity of the musicians and singers, the diversity of the arrangements. When I listened to the horns, it made me think differently about chords and how I played them on guitar. My dad's jazz records spoke to me in a way that pop and rock records could not, and I reacted strongly to that. It signalled a whole world of possibility to me as a musician.'

As he began to explore the recordings of less familiar jazz artists, a very broad universe of jazz opened up for Chris. New sounds thrilled him, such as Milt Jackson on the vibraphone out front of the Modern Jazz Quartet. Dave Brubeck playing complex time signatures on his hit song *Take 5*. The avant-garde compositions and unique phrasing of Charles Mingus, which opened the door to a broader appreciation of be-bop. The extraordinary musical dexterity of Louis Armstrong and his Hot Five band, which led to an appreciation of Miles Davis. The big, soulful voice of Ella Fitzgerald.

And providing the great bridge between all of these different musical flavours that appealed to Chris was Ray Charles, the dynamic rhythm and blues stylist who brought a jazzy swing to the backbeat and a wildness biting at the edge of his sweet vocal melodies. Chris took particular note of his 1959 hit *What'd I Say*, a song which would eventually feature in the set list of Chris's first band, St James Infirmary. 'That cool, slow swing got its hooks into me. It lit up the desire in me to play music, and it all came to me through listening to records – by taking a punt and listening to things that I wasn't familiar with.'

By comparison, Chris's reference point for British folk music was the definitive text *The Child Ballads*, a five-volume set of English and Scottish Popular Ballads that had been compiled by American Professor Francis James Child (first published in the 1860s), which Chris obtained in 1969. These were weighty tomes that stretched back to the 16th century, presenting daunting oral histories; a song such as *The Guest of Robin Hood*, for example, has 94 verses.

Chris's love of history made him persevere with dedicated learning of these epic folk songs. He became enamoured with the richness of the storytelling, and the vivid descriptions they painted of a distant time. 'I love how dramatic these old folk songs are. The violence, the lustiness, the big emotions and high passions. I found it all fascinating – and I certainly didn't think that me liking folk music was contrary or at odds with also exploring rock music, or blues or any other form of music.'

While many audiences know Chris primarily through his blues guitar playing, it's his passion for World Music, reflecting an appreciation of different cultures from around the planet, that plays a major part in shaping his musical ideas.

This stems from his eclectic collection of recorded music, and a restless desire to learn how different music is constructed and performed. When Chris first started hearing these exotic sounds in the late-1960s, the music of foreign cultures was originally termed Underground Music, and represented the most obscure items for record collectors to get their hands on – but Chris was insistent. He asked endless questions at import record shops to investigate music that was alien to him, and rewards came through his patience and persistence in the shape of rare recordings.

'I'm amazed now that the entire world of different musical cultures comes to our doorstep in Adelaide with the WOMADelaide festival, where more than 100 acts from around the world come to our city every year. I see young people having the opportunity to engage with all these musical cultures presented to them on a platter. Everything is available for them to taste and be inspired by whatever they choose. I'm delighted for them – but I'm also more than just a tad envious that it's now all so easy for them.'

The first African music to make a telling mark on Chris was the great South African singer Miriam Makeba and tin pennywhistle player Spokes

Mashiyane playing together on the song *Phatha Phatha*. 'I was only a kid listening to the radio, but the sound immediately struck me as unique. It was joyous, it was beautiful and it suggested to me that there was a whole universe of fantastic music out there that I had no idea about.'

However, it was an introduction to the music of Abdullah Ibrahim – the South African Jazz pianist and composer, who was also known as Dollar Brand – that represented a crucial turning point in Chris's musical life. 'Abdullah Ibrahim is among the biggest influences on me. Listening to him was a revelation, a life-changing moment that shaped my future in music. I kept thinking why hadn't I heard this incredible music before?'

He first heard of Abdullah through a recording session at ABC Adelaide studios in 1980 organised by Dave Woodhall, host of ABC Radio and TV program *Rockturnal*. Also present at this eclectic jam session was Nick Lyons (who played sitar, violin, viola and synthesiser) and Dave Kelly, a keyboard player from Sydney who had first been brought to Chris' flat at Mile End by Adelaide music promoter Peter Dawson. 'Dave Kelly told me he'd seen Abdullah Ibrahim play a solo piano gig at an arts factory in Nimbin, in northern New South Wales – and when I heard his recordings, it was the biggest musical upheaval that had ever happened to me. It completely changed the way I thought about music.'

The first Abdullah Ibrahim song that Chris learned was *Children of Africa*, and then *African Marketplace* – which Chris still plays in live performances (most recently as part of the *Live During Lockdown* DVD recorded with the Chris Finnen Band during 2021). It was the sum of so many complex yet complementary musical parts in Abdullah Ibrahim's music that affected Chris so greatly. 'It sounded like there were three people all playing at once, there was so much going on with how he played the piano, but it was always the melodies that were so satisfying. The incredible fusion of rhythmic and melodic content was earthy, deeply spiritual – yet it carried a very simple message of joy that could be conveyed without words. Once his songs got stuck in my head, I just couldn't get them out.'

The ABC *Rockturnal* session was also the first of Chris's recordings that involved long pieces with sitar improvisation. It was an instrument that first caught Chris's attention after hearing Ravi Shankar perform at the Monterey Pop Festival in 1967. 'I initially listened to that recording because I wanted to hear the songs Jimi Hendrix performed – and then I heard this incredible sitar that completely overwhelmed me for its fragile, hypnotic beauty. It was the polar opposite of what Hendrix did at the same festival.'

Then Chris heard The Beatles song *Within Without You* on the *Sgt Pepper's Lonely Hearts Club Band* album in 1967, and the exotic sounds of sitar, dilruba and tabla had him mesmerised. He began searching for the source music that had inspired George Harrison to write such a song.

'Any foray into Eastern music has been exciting to me – and when I first embarked on this journey it required a lot of effort to discover all the music I wanted. None of this music was freely available, nor was it very familiar to many people in Australia. I could only access the music through making acquaintance with someone knowledgeable in a record shop, and I would be buying albums on their advice. I trusted them implicitly, and even if I bought some records that I didn't like, I'd listen to them carefully, because I knew they had to offer something of merit if they had been recommended to me.'

Such recommendations included Ali Akbar Khan, the Bengali classical musician famed for his virtuosity in playing the sarod, a multi-stringed fretless Hindustani instrument that has the twang of a banjo but also the haunting waft of a drone. 'It was the peaceful sound of an Ali Akbar Khan CD that I had playing in the birthing room when my son Izaac was born. The sweet sound of the sarod and the sweet aroma of lemon oil in the air – those were the sensory influences that greeted Izaac into this world.'

Open to all influences

A fascination with Ali Akbar Khan led Chris to discover more virtuoso performers from across the sub-continent, including the great Indian tabla player Zakir Hussain, and the extraordinary Pakistani qawwali vocalist Nusrat Fateh Ali Khan. 'It proved to me that you don't have to understand the language that someone sings in to understand the message they convey. They taught me so much about truly listening to music, to hear its true meaning.'

Understanding reggae music came to Chris via other musical strains that he had first heard as a boy growing up listening to the radio in the UK – such as the jaunty sound of Bluebeat and the Calypso music of Trinidad and Tobago, both which reflected a growing West Indian community residing in London through the 1960s.

Chris remembers hearing the 1962 hit single *Calypso Gossip*, a novelty song by English comedian Bernard Cribbins, poking fun at gossiping middle-aged housewives, set to a bouncing Calypso rhythm. It was something that immediately tickled young Chris's fancy.

Another was Millie's *My Boy Lollipop*, a pioneering Bluebeat single that made its way onto commercial radio. It was the first record issued by Chris Blackwell's Island Records, which later became the powerhouse reggae label that introduced Bob Marley and The Wailers to the world. Chris followed the progress and output of Island Records, and became enthralled by the charismatic Bob Marley and the muscular sound of his skanking reggae.

'The bass playing was always incredible, but I was drawn to listen to the guitar parts. It sounded like the guitar was doing fuck all, but it had to be done in exactly the right spot or the song would sound entirely wrong. It was a very precise skill to get it right. I actually heard a lot of similarities between blues and reggae – especially the reliance on great feel to project the essential mood of the music. It was never just about the notes you played, but how you delivered them.'

His growing collection of reggae albums inspired Chris to start writing his own original reggae songs, such as *Rastaman Versus Uncle*

Sam in 1975, his nod to the ongoing political struggles between the Rastafarian cult of Jamaica and their overbearing American neighbours. This lengthy, meandering song, drenched in wah-wah effect on Chris's guitar, became a feature of gigs during the first incarnation of the Chris Finnen Offering.

A love of reggae bloomed further through Chris's friendship with guitarist Ross Hannaford, who had made his name in Daddy Cool but had embraced reggae with his mid-1970s Melbourne-based outfit Billy T, featuring Russell Smith on vocals and guitar (who Chris knew from his previous band Company Caine), bass player and singer Joe Creighton (who later became a mainstay of John Farnham's band) and drummer Mic Holden.

'I've always kept jamming with people to learn, and Ross would come over to my flat on South Road whenever he passed through Adelaide. I can remember when he arrived after returning from a visit to Jamacia, carrying an armload of reggae singles that he'd bought while he was there. He was so excited to share them. And he had these heads of dope that were as big as corn on the cob, and so we lit up this giant spliff, then turned the volume up. We both had our guitars strapped on so we could play along to the music and it was just bliss. We were like a couple of giddy schoolkids, just dancing around the room and playing along to these reggae songs without a care in the world. From that point on, reggae was always about having fun for me.'

Later during Hannaford's visit in 1977, Chris was invited to join a recording session with Billy T at ABC recording studios in Collinswood, playing a reggae version of a Finnen original song called *Lucas Aaron* (named after Chris's nephew). Curiously, this song would be performed in many different styles, and features as an acoustic ballad on the *Three Sixty Degrees* album recorded in 1997.

Even food from different cultures represents a significant influence in Chris's mind, and Adelaide's abundant markets and vast collation

Open to all influences

of muti-cultural restaurants and cafes has certainly satisfied Chris's great passions of food and cooking – which he admits is ironic, having been raised on a dreary English diet. 'Ah yes, England, where if the Brussels sprouts are grey and look something like a collapsed lung, then they must be ready.'

His taste buds were set alight soon after arriving in Australia. As a migrant kid who left home in his mid-teens, he made friends with many other migrants of different cultures, spent time in their family homes and was introduced to the home-cooked meals of many nationalities. Curries, in particular, set his imagination alight. 'I've never met a curry I didn't like,' offers Chris with a broad grin. 'The aromas are as exciting as the flavours. I especially love cooking curries, because it fills my house with fantastic smells.' One recipe he is particularly proud of is a cherished Mulligatawny soup, the staple of Tamil cuisine from southern India. Chris also fondly remembers his son Izaac furrowing his brow in deep concentration the first time he tasted Chris's Thai green curry, then nodding in appreciation.

'I've lived alone for much of my life, so I like to cook while I'm listening to music. I'm quite practical, so I'll make up big batches of food in one session, especially when there's a busy run of gigs coming up. The food must be pretty good, because a lot of my muso friends from other cities choose to stay with me while they're in Adelaide – probably because they'll be guaranteed a decent feed.'

This list of recipes concocted in the Finnen kitchen is long and diverse. Roast duck with roasted potato 'armadillos' (this is what his son Izaac likes to called scored half-potatoes that fan out when they are roasted), bread pudding for dessert, and soups of any stripe. 'I reckon I could eat soup every day of the year – it's so delicious – but where would the fun be in that?'

The one great unresolved recording project that Chris has not yet undertaken involves combining his love of food and music. 'I want to release an album that features 12 recipes with appropriate music attached to each dish — a raga with a curry, a Celtic reel with a stew. I could include the recipe for each dish in the album liner notes, which would also explain the cultural appropriateness of each song. It would be music that people could eat along to. How good would that be!'

Chapter 9
Folk and rock and blues and everything else

Chris Finnen has steadfastly refused to be pinned down to any single music style, and he refuses to be hemmed in by boundaries or constrictive expectations. People may know him best for playing blues, but there's much, much more that shapes his complete musical identity.

'I've never subscribed to what the Blues Police say – the musical snobs who say that blues music can only be played a certain way or else it's not authentic. Those critics are just like horses with blinkers on, unable to see the bigger picture of what's going on. I love music so much that I've never been affected by prejudices. And because I'm in love with all types of great music, I've never considered that other people wouldn't also like the same great sounds. Adhering to this philosophy has given me the freedom to play and try everything. I just don't see any barriers constraining my ideas.'

Still, Chris readily acknowledges that blues is an essential touchstone of his music. 'When it comes to the blues, I like its honesty – when it's played properly. I especially love acoustic blues, and because I grew up playing an acoustic guitar first, I always appreciate the physical effort involved in playing it.

Finnenisms

'To form my own musical identity, I've taken the music I like and learned to play it by listening carefully, but I always add my two pennies worth. The desire to create has always been in me.'

The hunger to improvise has steered what Chris plays on guitar to the very edge of stylistic boundaries – especially during live performances. 'It's interesting to try explaining improvisation. It occurs in the moment, and you have to know exactly where you are in the music, but also have a sense of abandonment at the same time. It takes much longer than you think to be able to arrive at that point. It demands a real command of the instrument, and being totally in tune with yourself.

'To be innovative as a musician, there isn't any one lightbulb moment, no single revelation that made me go Aha! It has taken a lot of time and patience to find the bridges between different musical cultures, but if you are careful and considered, you begin to hear the common links – for instance, the drones that underpin the music of so many different cultures, from Indian sitars to Scottish and Irish pipes, to Aboriginal didgeridoos. Then there's the open tunings that define the blues and Celtic airs. Listen hard and you hear the connections.'

The sum of all these parts works its way into Chris's original songs, with the tunes topped by lyrics that are sometimes profound, sometimes comical, often whimsical, but always honest and written without a seed of cynicism. Chris says the sentiments in his lyrics capture some essential Finnenisms.

> *Keep your oven warm, I like my pastry just right*
> *I like to taste good gravy every time I take a bite . . .*
> *Keep your jam tart sticky so I can lick my fingers clean*
> *I gotta taste your home cookin', if you know just what I mean . . .*
> *Don't you give me no junk food, it just don't satisfy at all*
> *Let me get my hands on your oven. I'll get down on my knees and crawl.*

Keep Your Oven Warm,
by Chris Finnen, 1997

'There aren't any hard and fast rules surrounding my musical creativity, except that I hate the keys of E flat and F. Other than that, I've found that inspiring sounds tend to translate very quickly from my imagination to my fingers.'

Chris says that through his dedicated regime of daily rehearsal, he has realised what he is capable of mastering, and where he must devote more time to learn and improve. 'I'll try everything, but I play very close attention to what doesn't work. I may seem fearless when I'm playing, but I'm not foolish. It's the sum of hours spent rehearsing away from the stage that enables me to figure out exactly what I can and should be playing on stage.

'I know I can't do everything. When I first heard John McLaughlin, I was blown away, but I knew I couldn't play like that. A friend in Melbourne said that after seeing McLaughlin perform in concert, he was going to give up playing guitar, but I wasn't defeated by seeing a supreme master at work. It just made me want to try harder. I love Robert Fripp, but I'll never be able to play like him – and that doesn't diminish my appreciation of the sounds that he makes and the technology that I'm fascinated by. There's always a line that divides everything you like and everything you play.'

One of the early creative hotbeds for Chris's exploration of wild electric guitar was the Chris Finnen Offering, which took flight during 1977 with its second line-up featuring Mick Ridge on bass guitar and Paul Turner on drums. It represented the type of explosive rock-fusion power trio that had been instigated by The Jimi Hendrix Experience and Cream. It also combined the sum of Chris's musical inspirations to that point, building on the blues and rock foundations he had laid down during his years of performing in Melbourne.

Two big influences on Chris's guitar playing at this time were Jimi Hendrix and Robin Trower, with their pyrotechnic solos informing long instrumental passages at the heart of many Chris Finnen Offering songs performed on stage. 'I went through so many phases, because I was influenced by so many great guitarists. They just consumed me.'

The power and passion of the band was intoxicating for everyone in the band's orbit – including a teenage David Sly, who tagged along to the band's weekend rehearsals (being a school friend of Mick Ridge's younger brother, Tony). They had access to a tiny room that was squirreled away in the middle of St Aloysius College, in the shadow of the Catholic Cathedral in Adelaide. A tiny, ancient Catholic nun was the caretaker, who unlocked the old wooden door with a huge brass key before an array of large Orange and Marshall amplifiers were hauled into the tiny room.

Young Sly was aghast at what followed. 'It was outrageously loud, but it was the ferocious, focused energy of the trio and the way Chris attacked his solos that was so electrifying. I expected to hear a band learning their songs, but instead it was like a concert performance in this tiny room, with Chris closing his eyes and seeming to disappear into another world, playing his guitar with his teeth, lifting it and playing it behind his head as the solos reached a crescendo. He was cultivating his showmanship in the safety of that rehearsal room, and I was absolutely mesmerised. I kept thinking how on earth was it possible that such world-class music was being created in a convent storeroom in Adelaide?'

In the late 1980s, the East-West fusion group Indian Pacific veered in a very different – and unique – musical direction, having evolved from a chance meeting of interesting minds. German-born Professor Michael Junius and Indian-born Dr Krishna Kumar were both practitioners in Ayurveda natural medicine and had formed the Australian School of Ayurveda in Adelaide during 1982. They were also talented multi-instrumentalists and experts in Indian Classical Music. By 1988, their music had been brought to the attention of Chris via Adelaide concert promoter Peter Dawson, who ran Sunstone concerts at venues including Woodville Town Hall.

Professor Junius was toying with the idea of fusing Indian music with other forms, had spoken to Peter Dawson, and they went to see Chris Finnen perform. Professor Junius decided that working in collaboration with Chris had potential, even though he thought Chris's show was far too loud and intrusive.

'We first met up as a trio to try out several musical ideas, which gelled quite well,' recalls Chris, 'so Michael and Krishna then expanded the idea to add drums and double bass, along with Michael playing his classical European instruments including viola da gamba and soprano saxophone. At this point it became a true cross-pollination of Western and Eastern musical ideas.

'I'd say Michael Junius was probably the most accomplished musician I have ever met, but I was able to bring ideas to him as well, because I had different experiences of how improvisation could be based on different musical sources. Michael gave me a lot of leeway with compositions and a lot of respect, but I felt very much like the junior partner in this arrangement – like a sorcerer's apprentice. He never treated me like that, but I felt very humbled to be making music with him.'

Working with Indian Pacific led to a bold crash course in Eastern musical education for Chris, but he was a keen and willing student and Professor Junius proved to be a very patient and informative mentor. 'I found that I could pick up the timing and the sound of much of the Indian music very quickly, but there were specific aspects that I found incredibly difficult and I kept making instinctive mistakes on some very intricate passages. Hitting obstacles like this was very different and challenging for me, because I never usually got stuck on musical pieces – but I had to remind myself that I was having to learn a new language, and it took time before I became fluent.'

Chris also found strong musical links that tied his blues-based musical experience to aspects of Indian music, which triggered a new rush of ideas for his guitar playing. 'The construction and improvisation within Indian Classical Ragas have many inherent qualities found in the blues – especially the spirituality and deep feeling. I learned as much about percussion from playing this music as I did about melody. I also learned about so many technical aspects, including bending notes. Western musicians tend to use vibrato to cover up bad intonation. In striking contrast, every Indian note is very specific, with each tone broken down into micro-tones. Every note makes a crucial point in a composition, so understanding this introduced me to a form of musical discipline that I just wasn't used to. I was hearing music through another culture, in a way that my own culture didn't hear.'

Pursuing an improvisational fusion of Western blues and rock music with Indian classical music became all-consuming for Chris. 'What I wanted to do with this musical collaboration was to find ways to make it accessible to all audiences.'

This notion progressed a step further with Dya Singh, an Adelaide Sikh musician who heard Chris perform with Indian Pacific and approached him with the idea to overlay electric guitar to his songs. 'I said yes to this offer because I just wanted to learn more about Indian music, and Dya Singh presented me with a chance to play a very different and particular style, using Indian scales and modes in a different context to what I was used to.

'First and foremost, Dya was a devout Sikh, so his music was built around his personal religious convictions, and it was sung in a different language that I couldn't speak. He would carefully explain to me what each of the songs were about, and from this I would try to play appropriate guitar phrases that fit the spiritual perspective. The music was also more folkloric-based than classical-based.

'I worked out a tuning on my guitar that was appropriate – it's designed around an open C chord – rather than playing a sitar for this music. I could build a drone from stumming, and also play the tabla part by tapping on the guitar body.'

Rather than having a formal education in Indian classical music, Chris was picking it all up by ear – and as an outsider coming fresh to this music, he could hear strange connections and bridges between different styles, of Celtic and Blues and Ragas all working around similar melodic patterns and tones.

All of this was captured much later in a seminal Chris Finnen album – *360 Degrees*, recorded over five days by Mick Wordley at his Mixmasters Studio in Blackwood and released in 1997 by The Crossing Record Company, a label created by Barossa winemaker and music enthusiast Rick Burge. It was designed as a recording that embraced all of Chris' varied musical inspirations in the one package – deliberately sidestepping his reputation as a blues maestro. 'I knew that Chris had this incredible album in him that was bursting with ideas, and that it would come together as a very good body of work,' says Rick.

The photo at the centre of the album artwork best illustrates its eclectic nature. It features Chris sitting contemplatively with a glass of Burge Family Winemakers' famed Draycott Shiraz, surrounded by an imposing arsenal of 24 instruments that Chris performed on the album, being a range of acoustic and electric guitars, Indian stringed instruments and all manner of hand drums and percussion.

In covering a gamut of musical styles across the album's 12 songs, Chris performed keystone compositions that had endured throughout his career – notably featuring Abdullah Ibrahim's *Children of Africa* and *African Marketplace*, and a third version of Chris' 1975 original composition *Lucas Aaron*, being a plaintive acoustic rendition far removed from Chris' previous psychedelic rock and reggae versions. He also performed a Michael Junius song, *The Duhn*, that reflected the Indian classical inspiration of their band Indian Pacific, plus a rowdy Scottish air written by Chris called *Highland Mist*, and a howling country blues original called *Blues in the Woodwork*, with Adelaide bluesman Greg Baker on harmonica. A bigger surprise was the inclusion of *Country*, a composition by improvisational piano master Keith Jarrett, and an arrangement of the traditional Welsh hymn *All Through the Night*.

The diversity of all this music on the album proved the vital selling point for Rick Burge to convince WOMADelaide festival director Rob Brookman that Chris Finnen should be included as a solo artist in the festival line-up for the first time in 1999 (Chris had previously performed at WOMADelaide in 1997 as a member of Dya Singh).

'I was so thrilled that Chris's mastery of so many musical cultures was going to be recognised at this globally-respected World Music festival,' recalls Rick, 'but when we got there, Chris got into a funk about only being scheduled to perform in one of the small tents. I kept saying he was finally being respected as a truly eclectic guitarist; Chris kept saying he deserved a more prominent stage to perform on.' It became a sore point between them that lingered, long after a full house in the WOMADelaide tent had rapturously received Chris's performance of material from the *360 Degrees* album.

Chris's eclectic music taste also proved to be the decisive factor in forming a strong musical performance relationship with Colin Offord, the extraordinary creator of unique musical instruments fashioned from found objects, and composer of startling original avant-garde compositions that highlight his innovative instruments. He is also the founder of The Great Bowing Company, an eclectic and shifting ensemble that comes together for tours to perform Colin's original music.

Colin and Chris initially came together in the late-1990s, to perform live music for Restless Dance Theatre, an Adelaide performance company for people with disability. Colin had been engaged to prepare a score and soundtrack for a show featuring only visually-impaired performers in Adelaide, and Chris was suggested as an appropriate musician to suit the project. 'I was introduced to Colin as a blues player and I don't think he was overly impressed by the limitations of that,' recalls Chris, 'but once we started talking about our musical interests, we realised that we both had an appetite for strange, unconventional music – and that formed a common bond between us. Colin started calling me to get involved in his touring projects, because we both realised there was so much unexplored space in his music where we could work together.'

Chris was immediately captivated by this music, featuring strange sounds produced by such instruments as Mouth Bow and Husk Bow, harmonic windpipes (flutes) and Moon Bells (a rack of suspended, heavy, crescent-shaped metal objects) played by Colin's Taiwanese wife Yilan Yeh (also a video artist, whose works feature as visual backdrops to Colin's live performances).

This presented the type of boundary-defying creative environment that Chris thrives in, says Colin, which is why they have worked together many times across two decades. 'Chris brings heart, soul, technique, ideas – he always has something interesting and of value to say in music,' says Colin.

Working on Colin's very idiosyncratic style of music demands significant input and focused performances from his musical colleagues, especially as Colin says he never tells anyone what to play. 'I start from the basis of exploring a sound, so any musician who comes to my projects has to have their own sound that they can apply to serve the music. Chris has this. The feel in his fingers, the way he touches the strings, it strikes at the essential emotive quality of music. I've heard him pick up a clapped-out old guitar and produce beautiful rich sounds from it. He embodies the music.'

Friendship also plays a crucial role in their working relationship. 'It's like resuming a conversation with an old friend whenever we play music together,' says Colin, who now lives in Melbourne. He says the test for whether he wants to work and tour with other musicians is to share a meal with them – to see if they can share interesting conversations and enjoy each other's company – and he says Chris passed this test with flying colours. It's a big part of why they still work together.

'Every time I receive an invitation to tour with Colin, I get excited, because I know I will learn something,' says Chris. 'With Colin, they are usually lengthy, very intensive runs of performances – with particular highlights being two performances at Government House in Sydney. The main show was in the old ballroom, but before this the musicians were placed at strategic points throughout the venue – some on staircase landings, some in the gardens, and I was sitting on beautiful antique furniture, playing improvised acoustic guitar as the audience absorbed this genteel atmosphere while enjoying tea, cakes and delicate snacks. That night, after the performance, Colin and I got to stay the night in the old butler's quarters.

'It was so very different for me to be under such strict direction from Colin, without being the band leader myself, but I still found it extremely invigorating. It was like structured improvising, following the lead of Colin's mouth bows, which were tuned to their own peculiar keys, so I'd have to tune my guitar accordingly, and often in very unconventional tunings that were completely foreign to me. I had to learn a lot of this in the moment, so there was no time to daydream. It was yet another valuable piece of my musical education.'

Chapter 10
The lessons learned from performing with others

'I like performing because I love being around people.' It has been this way since a 15-year-old Chris found the nerve to jump on stage for impromptu jam sessions with bands in Melbourne, and it remains a fundamental reason why Chris continues to perform regular gigs as he shuffles past his 70th birthday. He says a key appeal is the exhilaration of having to think and act in the moment.

'If I stumble, the world won't wait for me to catch up. The desire to communicate compels you to speak – through your lyrics, and through your instrument. It has changed quite a bit over the years, of course. I went through many different phases, because I was heavily influenced by so many musicians, and I was listening to music constantly. I can identify what every bit of my playing style has been inspired by – that's Rory Gallagher, that's Jimi Hendrix, that's Albert King – but then little bits come out that's just purely me. I first recognised this in the late-1980s and early 1990s, and I felt something really open up inside of me.'

> **I regard the music of the mid-1960s to the early-1980s as the most inspiring of my generation, and together with people having a broader embrace of different cultures and**

philosophies, it seemed that a lot of old boundaries were being broken down. Everything converged in a mixture of music, fashion, food, medicine, alternative lifestyles and art, and I felt energised by a general atmosphere of peace and tolerance towards all. If you really wanted to do something, the opportunity would generally present itself, and there were ways and likeminded people to get things happening. Sometimes it came together easily. Sometimes it required a lot of hard work.

In the psychedelic era, mind-expanding drugs played a part in shaping the consciousness of the time. For me, the idea of smoking hashish or taking LSD was a purposeful experiment in trying to expand my mind and find new dimensions of thought. There is no doubt that The Beatles' *Sgt Pepper* album, along with *Axis Bold As Love* and *Electric Ladyland* by Jimi Hendrix, provided a catalyst for this train of thought. I actually learned a great deal from this experimenting and I don't regret it. I believe your mind is something you choose to work with as you wish, but it's not the drugs that provide the answers. It's your personal motivation and constant work at what you do that provides the key to all your mental or physical achievements.

His years spent working with the Matt Taylor Band saw Chris amplify his sense of showmanship during performances. 'Matt and I ended up having this really strong telepathy between us, and that translated especially well on stage. Matt and I worked together really well as a team by being dual frontmen, with me being especially animated as I played guitar. It wasn't a contrived thing that we worked out during rehearsal. It just developed in the moment on stage. There was a lot of spontaneous madness happening, and that made the shows especially exciting for the audiences. Matt would open up his stance and I'd dive through his legs. I'd be jumping off speaker stacks, all done with absolutely no athletic skill whatsoever. That's probably why my back is so stuffed now, as a consequence of all those antics.'

Antics included a lot of pranks and practical jokes while on tour, which Matt remembers would often spiral out of control, thanks to Roy Daniel who played bass in the Matt Taylor Band. 'Roy was the great practical joker, and I warned Chris about him, but that only made Chris seem to rise to the challenge,' says Matt. 'With his limited visibility, Chris became the perfect target for Roy, who would start water pistol fights that would escalate into water balloon fights, then end up with buckets of water dropping from hotel bedroom doorways. Eventually I'd have to step in and say "Enough!". It's not easy trying to run a band on tour with a lot of bored musicians having too much spare time on their hands each day.'

Roy's pranks kept mounting up: anchovies being hidden inside Chris's guitar cases, beds being short-sheeted, or dusted with a layer of talcum powder or shelled boiled eggs. Chris also remembers Roy changing the numbers on the door of his hotel room in Sydney. 'When we finished the gig and got back to what I thought was my room, the key didn't fit, so I went back to the reception desk to explain my problem,' says Chris. 'Of course, by the time I'd returned with the hotel manager, the numbers had been changed back and my key opened the door perfectly, leaving me very red-faced trying to explain myself to the manager.'

An integral part of Chris's stage persona has been parading his wardrobe of outrageous colourful clothing – which some would say are brought together in quite ludicrous combinations – and this has been a Finnen signature from his earliest days of performing. 'Right from the outset, I was influenced by the look of Jimi Hendrix, and then the Sgt Pepper-era Beatles. The whole fashion scene of London in 1967-68 excited me, and I especially loved the wild colours. Mum was sympathetic to my taste; she got some psychedelic lime green material and made a wide tie for me. I'd wear it when I first started performing on stage.

'I always made the effort to dress up for a performance, because I considered that an important part of putting on a show for the audience. I would never wear the colourful clothes because I wanted to look ridiculous. It was because I wanted to entertain people in every way, shape and form.

'The psychedelic fad passed, but my love of those wild, colourful clothes has never waned. Sure, people razz me about it, but ultimately, I can see that it makes a lot of people happy. And quite often, some of those seemingly random combinations of clothes actually go together!'

His flamboyant look would be further enhanced by an ever-changing array of hairstyles, thanks to his next-door neighbour at Mile End during the 1970s and 1980s, the hairdresser and renowned drag queen Roger Shepherd. 'I had teased-out afros, long scraggly curls, fringes, but also beards and moustaches trimmed in all manner of shapes, and then the facial hair would disappear altogether. It was a lot of fun, and it always kept things interesting.'

Bandmates would often shake their heads in disbelief at some of Chris's costumes. Matt Taylor would announce to his audiences that he was in a band that was supporting Chris Finnen's wardrobe. Still, Matt would often accompany Chris on shopping sprees in the Paddington Markets when the band visited Sydney, with Chris invariably buying lurid clothes that would end up being his costume for that evening's performance.

'I had one particularly outrageous jacket that I wore throughout a Matt Taylor Band tour, purposely trying to get a rise out of the band, and the guys became thoroughly sick of it, so they hid it in one of the hotels when we had to leave town, and we kept travelling up the east coast of Australia. When we came back to the same hotel two weeks later, the lady at reception said she was relieved to see me. "You left your jacket behind, so we've had it dry cleaned and here it is, ready for you to wear for your performance tonight." I got the last laugh on that occasion.'

The lessons learned from performing with others

As a great fan of jazz, Chris was excited and a little overwhelmed to be granted an impromptu performance with veteran Australian jazz guitarist George Golla in Adelaide during the early 2000s. During the first half of his show, Golla asked the audience if they had any requests, which prompted Chris to call out for the Anthony Newley ballad *Who Can I Turn To*. Impressed by such a tasteful request, Golla's manager recognised Finnen and went to him during interval, suggesting that the two guitarists could perform together and trade solos during a song in the second set. 'At first, I was flabbergasted by the invitation – and then once I joined him on stage I was floored again because George started the song in the key of F, which is my least favourite key to improvise on. I did the initial part of my solo very correctly, very politely, out of respect, but in time I made a conscious decision to go further, to let him know a little bit more about me. He gave me a smile, picked up where I was going and took it further. What a thrill! I only wish I had a recording of that magic moment.

'When you perform on stage with other people, it really is about pushing yourself further – having the confidence to express your own personality through what you play.'

Saying yes to one interesting musical opportunity often led to another fantastic musical venture. The success of Chris's collaboration with Professor Michael Junius and Krishna Kumar led to their fusion group Indian Pacific being invited to perform for the Dalai Lama during his visit to Adelaide in 1992. The Evening with the Dalai Lama concert was conducted on May 2 at the Adelaide Entertainment Centre, and Indian Pacific performed the original composition *Messenger of Peace*, which Professor Junius had written when he visited the World Meditation Centre in New York City, a side-venture while he attended a medical conference in the same city. Professor Junius wrote the piece on a shawm, a double-reed woodwind instrument, and constructed the music around a Tibetan scale, serving as a homage to the homeland of the Dalai Lama.

The Dalai Lama was so moved by the Indian Pacific performance of this composition that he stood up and crossed the stage to thank Michael Junius – a rare honour. The group was then given front row seats, to listen to the Dalai Lama's oration. 'When the Dalai Lama started talking, I almost started chuckling because to my ears, he sounded just like Yul Brenner in *The King and I*, which is a movie our family had seen so many times when I was a young kid,' says Chris. 'I wasn't being disrespectful, but it just struck me as amusing and I had to keep stifling a laugh.'

Playing before the spiritual deity was a momentous occasion for Chris. 'I was nervous with excitement but not fear.' For the performance, Chris was not even playing his familiar guitar. Instead, he played a tambura – a long-necked, four-stringed instrument that provides a continuous harmonic drone. 'I like the subtleness and understatement that this instrument brings to the music. It's a hollow instrument, and you can feel its vibrations through your chest. For the Dalai Lama performance, I played one of two tamburas in the group. It sounded as though we had created a sea of sound on which the other instruments could project various ideas. It transported me to another place, and I was very reflective during this performance. My dad had died only a short time before, so I found the moment very peaceful and transformative – and this was a very big lesson for me to learn, because it's essentially the opposite of what rock music does.'

Chris has since used tambura in many of his recordings – and due to his Scottish heritage, Chris says he understands the power of the drone in music. 'Yes, there's the sound of bagpipes in my heritage, but I always say the first drone you ever hear is a mother-in-law ... but seriously, the drone is a mesmerising sound. I think that subconsciously, the drone sound affects us all profoundly.'

Virtuoso blues guitarist Jeff Lang became another of Chris's significant musical allies. Ironically, they first met after a 20-year-old Jeff ('Still a very green and slightly wild lad from Geelong,' he remembers) had taken over Chris's role as guitarist in the Matt Taylor Band. 'It was in 1989, when the band was playing in Adelaide, and Matt insisted that we go out after our gig to hear Chris playing the after-midnight shift at The KoKlub in Hindley Street,' says Jeff. 'Matt's a wise old soul, and he could tell that we'd hit it off. It was a thrilling introduction, because while his onstage demeanour was the antithesis of self-important strutting, the *sounds* that Chris was pulling from his guitar betrayed decades of serious musical obsession and study. I could hear the influences of players I loved, such as Roy Buchanan, Ry Cooder, John Lee Hooker and Peter Green, but those had clearly been thoroughly absorbed and were now expressed as part of his own vocabulary on the instrument, not merely recycled.

'In addition, he was blending in a world of influences outside of my own listening experience at that point: African musical patterns, Indian inflections, Celtic melodies. I was knocked out by what he was playing, so I hung around afterwards and picked up a guitar – and we ended up jamming until 7.30am!'

The high point of their combined musical output was captured in a live recording of a concert they performed together at Burge Family Winemakers cellar door, at Lyndoch in the Barossa Valley, in May 1996. Winemaker and winery owner Rick Burge had provided the impetus and resources to make this recording possible. He had met Chris through organising blues gigs at the Wheatsheaf Hotel in East Gawler. Called the Crossing Blues Club, it involved Rick and Barossa musician Tony Luke bringing blues and acoustic musicians into the Barossa region for regular gigs. Through this initial connection, Rick booked Chris to perform at a major event he was helping to organise for the 1995 Barossa Vintage Festival – Lyndoch Uncorked, a large food, music and wine affair held on Lyndoch Oval. To add some extra spice to his acoustic performance, Chris invited Jeff Lang to join him on stage.

'There was a special electricity between them – the magic of the six-string and 12-string guitar combination. I was completely knocked out by what I was hearing,' says Rick. 'I wanted to hear more, but there was no recording of them playing together, so I rather naively asked both of them if we could do another show and record it. Jeff Lang's manager, John Sinclair, initially dismissed me as a bit of a greenhorn, but I then organised a special fund-raising gig for Faith Lutheran College in the Barossa at very short notice, and it was a resounding success, so his opinion of me changed after that. He became very enthusiastic about Jeff being involved in my idea for a live recording.'

Rick made contact with recording engineer Mick Wordley of Mixmasters Studio in Blackwood – largely because he knew that Wordley had won Best Sound Engineer at the SA Music Industry Association awards. Mick arrived at the winery with his 24-track mixing desk and transformed a big marquee adjacent to the Burge Family Winemakers cellar door into a recording location.

Five acts were booked to perform at Rick's winery in Lyndoch across Saturday 27 April and Sunday 28 April, 1996, including Adelaide jazz singer Libby Donovan accompanied by pianist Sheree Dunsford (now Sheree Sullivan, proprietor of Udder Delights cheese manufacturers), plus singer/multi-instrumentalist John Francis and Tony Luke. Chris and Jeff had their performances from both days recorded, and gifted multi-instrumentalist Kerryn Tolhurst (previously of The Dingoes, and on a fleeting return visit to Australia from New York) came along and sat in for a few songs. The inspired live recording featured no overdubs.

'It was a perfect day. Everyone played superbly, the audience loved it,' says Rick. 'The wine flowed, and we had organised for the Star of Siam Restaurant, a longstanding Thai restaurant based in Gouger St, Adelaide, to come on site and do the catering. Everyone was very happy, and I think that came through on the recording.'

With the resulting tapes meeting everyone's approval, Rick formed his own recording label, The Crossing Record Company, to issue the disc *Finnen & Lang: Live at the Vineyard*. It registered good sales and very strong reviews around Australia. It also won a legion of new fans, as Chris learned years later when he played a solo gig at Taree, in northern New South Wales. A young woman came up to Chris and requested one of his original compositions, *Trouble No More*. She had purchased the *Finnen & Lang: Live at the Vineyard* CD from Jeff Lang when he had performed in Taree, and she worked in the local kindergarten. 'She would play my song to the little children during their early afternoon sleep time,' says Chris. 'What a wonderful way for my song to be used!'

The musical sympatico that grew through Chris and Jeff's friendship led them to do more touring together, which had them constantly pushing each other's musical boundaries. Chris laments that he wasn't much help through being unable to do driving stints during these long hauls between regional gigs – 'poor Jeff had to haul me along as freight: One carcass, prime English beef,' quips Chris – but they at least shared a lot of prime listening time in the vehicles.

'We were always playing each other the latest music that each of us had encountered. It was a fabulous exchange; Jeff turning me onto whatever he was excited about, and me doing the same for him,' says Chris. 'We spent so much time on the road together and music was being played in the van continuously as we travelled from gig to gig, so my musical education was constant. Those influences ultimately rub off. Of all my musical friends, I'd say that Jeff's ferocious appetite for listening to a huge variety of new music from all walks of life is probably closest to mine.'

Chris remembers making the most of any difficult situation when he toured with Jeff. At a pub in Blacktown, a tough part of Sydney's inner western suburbs, they found their PA system was no more than a weedy DJ console, and a single microphone with no stand. They taped the mic to a broom stick and stood it in a mop bucket, turned up the volume and Chris started playing, so that a weary Jeff could eat a meal after his long day of driving to reach the gig on time. 'Hello, I'm Chris Finnen from Adelaide,' he announced cheerfully. 'Why don't you fuck off back there,' came a booming reply from one punter, before a single note had been played. 'It inspired me to start flailing my guitar from the word go,' recalls Chris, 'and I kept the energy going until Jeff joined me. We ended up having them dancing in a line behind us, Pied Piper-style, out into the car park. That was a night when our performing skills turned everything around for us – which is just as well, or otherwise they probably would have killed us.'

There were always plenty of antics to report from Finnen-Lang gigs: at Boyd Kelly's R&B Club in Canberra, Chris smoking out the dressing room with the greasiest bacon-and-egg cook-up, then Jeff happily eating the lot out of the pan on stage; Jeff interrupting one of Chris's solos at a Barossa Valley gig by winding him up 'Egyptian mummy-style' with transparent packing tape ('Lang 1: Finnen 0,' recalls Chris with a wry grin); an Adelaide University gig set up with a huge sound system that only attracted about 10 people, so Chris and Jeff grabbed their acoustic guitars and sat at tables next to the punters and played directly to them.

Jeff recalls their touring exploits with a smile. 'You couldn't ask for a more enjoyable touring companion. Chris is simply so funny, quipping and joking constantly, making the long drives fly past in a blur of puns, plus endless *Simpsons* and *Ren and Stimpy* quotes. For a guy who is deeply caring and soulful, he sure doesn't mind being silly, and that's a winning combination in a touring musician, in my view.'

Beyond the larks, there was also perfect unison that grew between this duo. At Sawtell RSL in Northern New South Wales, they arrived fatigued from travelling and hurriedly wrote out three songs each on blank pages to create a set list. They immediately went on stage and the show threaded together seamlessly. 'It's funny how all this works in your favour after years of shared experience,' says Chris.

Thanks to Jeff, Chris was presented with the opportunity to perform as a guest at the 2005 World Expo in Nagoya, Japan. 'The organisers of the Australian pavilion wanted someone to represent South Australia at the Expo. They had already invited Jeff to represent Victoria, so his manager suggested me as a worthy candidate. After being accepted, I flew to Singapore and met with Jeff before we caught a connecting flight to Nagoya for a week of gigs in the Australian pavilion at the Expo site.' They also enjoyed one day off from performing, taking the Shinkansen Bullet Train to Tokyo, for a whirlwind tour of the city's famed blocks of guitar shops (and buying crazy Japanese lollies for Chris's son Izaac and his school friends), plus enjoying sushi and sake on board the train during the return journey.

Jeff and Chris exchanged songs at each gig that they performed as a duo at the World Expo, but Chris was taken aback at how discrete and polite the Japanese audiences were. 'We had little idea whether they liked the performances or not. They were very reserved and rather non-committal, except for an old lady who gave a decorative painted fan to Jeff after our last gig. I did play a tune called *Cherry Blossom*, just so the Japanese audience could see that I had bothered to learn a Japanese tune.'

Chris also performed a racy acoustic guitar version of *Waltzing Matilda* using a slide that made it sound like a revved-up blues. 'I wanted to underline the reason why I was representing Australia at this event, but I wasn't going to bother anyone by trying to sing this song – the lovely melody says it all, as far as I'm concerned.'

> **It doesn't matter whether I'm playing at a big outdoor concert, a front bar, a winery, a stadium or around a kitchen table, I make music to share with people, to offer my spirit and to give the very best that I can. You can spend hours and hours on the road trying to get to a gig, and can be totally worn out when you arrive, but once you get on the stage, the energy finds you and the reason why you're playing becomes crystal clear. It doesn't matter whether there are 10 people in that audience or thousands, when you walk out on stage you have to realise that you are blessed and that you have this golden opportunity to make something happen that you can enjoy with everyone.**

Such enjoyment can occur anywhere – at weddings, funerals, hospitals, old-age homes, kindergartens and schools. 'These are all places that depend on strong community involvement, and through playing music in all these places, I've learned that music is the medicine of the common man. It's not all about having to enjoy some sort of commercial gain. If there's money available, I'll gladly take it, but if there's isn't any money, I'll happily do the show, provided someone can drive me to and from the location.'

> **Funerals are the most difficult places to play music, and while it's not something you really want to do, I've felt conclusive proof that music at a funeral can provide solace and spiritual comfort – and that's more than enough reason to accept an invitation to play. I vividly recall playing at my father's funeral. We were standing by the graveside in the rain, and I was staring at my mother, sister, auntie and uncle, trying to play my best as I thought about my father. I was told afterwards that I did a good job, but I was so nervous that my left hand was shaking uncontrollably. Well, Dad, that was the best vibrato and sustain that I've ever played with, so I'm pleased that it helped my dear family in such a sad moment.**

Chris also remembers an especially moving bedside vigil for his Latvian friend Zarnie Jaugietis, when he played guitar with Guy Cundell in the final hours of her battle with cancer. 'She couldn't talk, couldn't open her eyes, but she gestured that the music was comforting her. I took a cab home, and two hours later she was dead. I can only hope, in that moment, music provided some peaceful medicine.'

> *All my friends are going down that lonesome road*
> *They're going to meet their maker, and some of them just ain't that old ...*
> *I've seen people go out bravely, even though I know they're scared to death*
> *And I've seen people hang right on until they had nothing left.*

The lessons learned from performing with others

If you truly love your life, then love your family and all your friends
'Cause they're gonna be the ones left cryin''
When your life comes to an end.

All My Friends (Are Going Down That Lonesome Road),
by Chris Finnen, 2015

The opposite type of emotional outpouring occurs at weddings and engagement parties, as complete happiness and celebration fills the room. 'I sometimes wonder about being asked to play rhythm and blues at these occasions, because the lyric content doesn't usually have much to do with successful, long-term relationships,' says a bemused Chris. 'I like to play a heartfelt solo improvisation while the bride and groom are signing the register – something that you make up on the spot but is so personal, so deep that it's a special gift from you.'

However, Chris sometimes has to contend with uninvited and unwanted guests on stage. He remembers a gig many years ago at The Governor Hindmarsh Hotel in Adelaide, when a very large, very inebriated lady suddenly jumped out of the audience. 'She proceeded to do the Dance of the Seven Army Surplus Blankets, but she was spinning perilously close to a rack of very expensive guitars,' says Chris. 'Fortunately, I had about 25-feet of guitar cable at my disposal, so I started playing my guitar one-handed, put my other arm around this woman and danced her over to the steps at the side of the stage. I was very relieved that she was satisfied with her 10 seconds of glory.'

Open-air festival stages present their own interesting set of challenges. 'Well, there's always the wind blowing the sound around; Mother Nature's great phase shifter, as I call it. Playing directly into the hot sun in summer isn't a great idea, and electricity and rain don't come together in a very safe manner, either.'

He remembers playing at an open-air blues festival on Hahndorf Oval, organised by Adelaide blues musician Greg Baker, and during his solo acoustic blues set, a curvaceous girl walked onto the stage and began to remove all her clothing. Chris acknowledges this was a rather spectacular intrusion, but somewhat awkward and inappropriate for a gentle Sunday afternoon acoustic set played in front of a family audience...

> **The stage is a place that I believe a musician has to respect. Not only is it your workplace, but I say it's sacred ground. Sure, you can invite guests onto the stage to make your performance special and provide a nice surprise for the crowd, but most of the time these moments are planned or discussed beforehand. There can also be impromptu invitations. I've certainly been fortunate enough to be in a club without a guitar, only to have one handed to me by the artists on stage and included in an impromptu jam.**
>
> **But it bothers me that some people take it upon themselves to climb up on stage without being invited. Harmonica players are the worst, running to the nearest microphone and sucking and blowing for all they're worth. Mostly, I'd say they suck. All you can do is keep playing until they run out of ideas and stop playing... and that usually doesn't take very long.**

And when things go wrong, as they invariably do, a smart musician is quick to react. Chris remembers the power going out on many occasions – which led to candles being lit on tables at a suburban Adelaide pub while Chris continued playing an acoustic set, and a tent gig in McLaren Vale that was saved by a guy driving his car to the entrance and leaving his headlights on while Chris picked up his metal-bodied resonator guitar and kept singin' the blues.

There are also the glorious spontaneous moments when serendipity is definitely working in your favour. 'I was playing a solo acoustic set at the Goolwa Folk Festival, and had just launched into an old Hambone Willie Newburn song called *Rollin'n'Tumblin'*. It features bottleneck slide guitar that imitates the sound of a steam train, and in that moment The Cockle Train, a heritage steam-powered tourist train, went roaring along the tracks located right next to the venue. The driver blew the train's whistle. I answered it on the guitar. Talk about spontaneous combustion...'

It's much more enjoyable when gigs are well organised, such as The Groove Garden in McLaren Vale, run by noted music photographer and devoted music fan Samra Teague. 'She's such a strong-willed woman with a deep understanding of community spirit,' says Chris. 'This gig would encourage up-and-coming musicians to get on stage and jam with established guest musicians, and then a feature act would perform. There would be beautiful home-cooked food served throughout the day, and these Sunday afternoons were such wonderful events where everyone shared a truly joyful experience. That's a prime example of music's power in bringing people together.'

Chapter 11
Parenthood

While music and playing guitar shape Chris's creative essence, it is parenthood that makes Chris most proud. His deep love for his son Izaac and the journey they have travelled together is the sunshine that radiates through Chris Finnen's story.

Music certainly plays its part in this big chapter of Chris's life. 'When my son was only half an hour old and still in the birthing unit, and he was laying on the bed beside his mother, I started playing guitar, just some improvised strumming in open-G tuning, but it brought something truly beautiful into the room, and the nurse was moved to tears. Music can say so much in a moment, when no words are necessary.'

When Chris and Izaac's mother separated, Chris took on sole parenting duties. Although he was initially daunted by the prospect of raising a two-year-old boy in his Seaford Rise home, Chris was bolstered by the encouragement and support of many friends. 'I rang my mum and my aunty for a lot of advice, but Izaac and I largely muddled our way through, and we did things together. The relationship I have with Izaac is incredibly close as a result.'

Parenthood

It goes without saying that Chris was an unorthodox parent. 'My father was a very strict, rather gruff Scotsman – and I didn't want to be like that with my son. I wanted to give Izaac freedom and leeway to make many of his own choices, but I always had discussions to make him aware of outcomes and fair consequences. I was upfront with him about my difficulties. I told him that I didn't have a parenting guidebook to follow, so we were on the journey together.'

It wasn't easy for a working musician to be the sole carer for a young child, with Chris's work hours demanding that he be away from home for many evenings. He had great support from a mother at the local day care centre, who would take Izaac for overnight sleeps, but would have to drop him home at 7am the following morning on her way to work. 'It was a rather unconventional set-up but we made it work. I'd tell Izaac when he got home early in the morning that we'd play a game called Zombiac, and I was the Zombiac. That that's how I felt staggering around the house with only a few hours' sleep after a gig.'

Because Chris could not drive a car, the father and son would walk through their neighbourhood to All Saints Primary School at Seaford Rise each morning, no matter the weather. 'If it was raining, we'd jump in puddles and splash each other and laugh, then have hot chocolate when we got home. We had to do things differently to the other kids, but I tried to make it fun.'

Chris would volunteer at Izaac's school to present musical education workshops. 'It really used to bother me that musical education had been pushed into the back seat at schools, far behind sports as an activity for children, so I wanted to give the kids some musical interaction. I worked with the headmistress to develop a program called Building Musical Bridges Between Cultures, and this worked well, because I pointed to a map of the world and introduced the kids to music from so many different places, working in the history and stories of each culture as we played the tunes.

'It was so nice that children sent me letters explaining how much they enjoyed this experience, and then, sometime later, I found out that some of them had taken this initial love of music much further. In that moment, I realised I had fulfilled my duty to pass on the joy of making music. This type of music education doesn't come from a book. It's all about brain power and open ears, motivation and practise.'

One activity the father and son cherished was bedtime stories read aloud, for which Chris would always apply a different accent to the voice of each different character. 'The only accent I could never do was an Australian accent, oddly enough,' offers Chris. 'Whether it was *Alice in Wonderland* or *Wind in the Willows*, everyone in the story got an accent, and Izaac would always roll about laughing. Even when he had friends stay over, he would always insist – "Do the accents, Dad" – and his friends weren't the least bit interested, but he always loved my silly performances. I reckon the accents probably came out of me loving the *Goon Show*, and Izaac now has that same love of hearing the beauty of voices and language.'

Music was also a big part of Izaac's home life, not only with records constantly playing through the stereo system and Chris forever practising on one of the dozens of guitars dotted about the house, but also with his exposure to frequent group rehearsals. 'When other musicians would rehearse at our house, I'd always extend some hospitality by bringing out a tray of snacks to share. So, whenever anyone would come over and started playing music, Izaac would appear and ask "Dad, can I bring out the snacks now?" I think it was often because he wanted to get into the blue cheese, but it was a good lesson that he learned to always share what you have with others.'

Once Izaac was deemed old enough, from the age of about 10, Chris began taking him on tours, most often during school holidays. When tour schedules did intrude on school time, Chris would set Izaac tasks during their travels, including writing diaries about what they did, and visiting museums in the towns where they stayed. 'I tried to make touring a life education lesson for him. It wasn't easy. It wasn't always comfortable, either. Sometimes we had to share a bed together, often we slept on friends' couches, but we experienced so much from spending time with so many different people, from so many different walks of life.'

It wasn't all hardship on the road, though. 'I remember when Izaac first tasted crème brulee when I played a gig at the Brisbane Jazz Club. He certainly loved special food and he got to taste a lot of it in the venues where I performed.'

This is evident in a tour diary Chris kept in 2012, when he travelled with Izaac to Queensland for a series of gigs with Colin Offord, which began on Monday 9 January: 'packed our bags, guitars, skateboard, etc...'

> **Tuesday 10:** We go to a Gold Coast coffee shop and Izaac orders a huge breakfast – bacon, eggs, sausage, beans, toast, mushrooms, tomatoes and a flat white coffee. Later we take the 45-minute ferry trip to Macleay Island and settle into Colin's house, with two curlews standing in the garden to greet us...
>
> **Wednesday 11:** Izaac goes to Mudflat Mangrove Beach with Colin for a swim. It's a nice way for Izaac to get to know Colin. They both come back talking nine to the dozen. They are great together. Izaac informs me later that he likes Colin because he's such a laid-back character – but Izaac doesn't have to go through Colin's demands as a musical director. Still, when it comes to rehearsing, Colin is a diligent but very humane task master.
>
> **Thursday 12:** We are on Coochiemudlo Island preparing for our first concert, and Izaac is up a ladder, helping to hang sails from large trees around a lagoon that will have Yilan's movies projected onto them. Afterwards, Izaac leads me by torchlight on a walk around the lagoon, and discovers hundreds of cane

toads – which everyone tells him to kick like a football, and kill as many as possible. It's much nicer for us to look at the ghostly torchlight profiles of curlews walking with their strange gait in this island paradise.

Friday 13: Each day now starts with Izaac and Colin having a swim at the beach. Izaac devours another huge meal. The boy's stomach must be endless. I'll have to start calling him The Locust. After sundown, he does the rounds with the torch, finding green tree frogs and large geckos all over the ceiling, including one translucent one. Izaac points out that he can see its internal organs and heart beating.

Saturday 14: To help prepare for the concert, Izaac is helping to lay out the sound cables and is learning how a PA system works. He leads me to the stage in the dark, helps me pack up my gear, and then The Locust finds the band's backstage meal of ham glazed with honey, marmalade and Dijon mustard that has been cooked for three hours. I feel very satisfied – a beautiful place, evening and music, a beautiful son.

Monday 15: Colin prepares a wood barbecue on his front verandah, with T-bone steaks and Chinese greens. Colin and Izaac keep sharing jokes in exaggerated Queensland accents, and their laughter rings out in the night. Ah, the joys of life. Everyone is very impressed with Izaac and agree he is a wonderful boy.

Wednesday 18: Colin introduces The Locust to the joys of crème caramel – a beautiful dessert for a beautiful young man – and as Izaac nods his approval, Colin is beaming with 'I told you so' happiness.

Thursday 19: We do our final packing and head back to Brisbane, then a long drive back to the Gold Coast. It brings back old memories of my touring days with Matt Taylor, but now I have Izaac falling asleep on my shoulder in the back seat of the car, while the stereo system loudly pounds out Tom Waits songs. After so much activity on this tour, Izaac has hit the wall and remains in a deep sleep.

Izaac's main passion is skateboarding, but he can play several musical instruments, and Chris proudly recalls when Izaac joined him on stage for two gigs in Melbourne to play drums, accompanying Chris for *House of the Rising Sun* as a tribute in memory of the late Dutch Tilders – and won a roar of approval from the audience. 'Izaac was very shy about playing in front of people, but he knows and feels music implicitly. I'll never forget that performance with him. Every time we get to play *House of the Rising Sun* and dedicate it to Dutch, it's a good thing for both of us.'

Chris was chuffed that Izaac acknowledged Chris in his 21st birthday speech, praising him for 'being the only one who's always been there for me... and thanks for all the dinners'.

Chapter 12
Tour . . . record . . . tour

The reputation forged by Chris Finnen through 55 years of performing and recording has led to him sharing a stage with a host of international luminaries – including Buddy Guy, Bo Didley, Jimmy Witherspoon, Roy Buchanan, Eric Burdon, Keb' Mo', Bob Brozman, Johnny Copeland, The Holmes Brothers, John Mayall and Mavis Staples.

It has also taken him on a long meandering trek throughout Australia, forming enduring friendships with the likes of Dutch Tilders, Phil Manning, Matt Taylor, Jeff Lang, Gwyn Ashton, Margret RoadKnight, Kevin Borich, Rob Riley and Colin Offord.

Yet despite all this, Chris still shies away from boxing his musical personality into a rigid definition. 'I can't tell you what Australian blues is – but I know it when I hear it. It's a bit like trying to describe what a watermelon tastes like to a Martian. Where do you start?'

Living a life on the road with vision impairment hasn't been easy for Chris. His problems were compounded during the 1980s, where a severe vitreous haemorrhage left him blinded for about two years, but fortunately vision returned in his good eye. 'My vision problems have been intermittent, and that has confused a lot of people. I would simply always do my best.'

To continue performing through this difficult period, Chris had to plan work-around issues.

On stage, the lighting would be turned down low, and he would take his own square of carpet to mark out a space where it was safe for him to stand. At home, he would modify the control knobs of his amplifiers with a metal file, to cut notches that would identify his preferred settings.

'At this time, I didn't panic that I couldn't see things, because I used my other senses more acutely. It made me focus on the pure sound of my guitar tones. I think it actually made me understand my playing style more through having to concentrate so hard.'

Chris's great passion for eating well saw him make pragmatic decisions while packing ahead of the Matt Taylor Band's second national tour in 1982 – adding an electric frypan and several Tupperware containers into his suitcase. 'I initially copped a ribbing from the rest of the band, but that changed once we started playing in country towns and there was nowhere open after we'd finished the gig. I'd go back to my room and start cooking up things in my frypan, and soon enough all the other band members would follow the smells and start drifting by at about 3am hoping to scrounge some food.'

Chris remembers touring as a fun time of adventure and exploration. 'By the end of a tour, I'd always come home with an extra bag filled with new clothes, new books and records. Everywhere I'd go, I would plug into something new.'

His other great touring companion was a portable cassette player and a set of headphones, so that whenever he wasn't playing, he was still listening to music and being inspired. 'With a cassette player, I could also record bits and pieces and catalogue my ideas. I'd never get to play these in the Matt Taylor Band – they just didn't fit – so I'd store them away for another time, when I was playing my own music again. That process of always thinking about and considering lots of different music has never stopped.'

Being on the road with the Matt Taylor Band through the mid-1980s and playing to a national audience for the first time was a dream come true for Chris.

'It was intensive. We were playing every night, sometimes three gigs in a night, and they started to take a toll on my fingertips. I was also playing every morning in my hotel room to rehearse – and I even gave lessons in my hotel room. People would come up to me at gigs and ask me to teach them things on the guitar, so I'd have them come around the next morning at 11am and give them a lesson. It was non-stop guitar.'

Despite the frequency of playing so much guitar, Chris noted that Matt Taylor stuck with the same set list throughout every tour. 'Because we were playing exactly the same songs night after night, the band got incredibly tight – but as a player I'd have to find ways of challenging myself. I'd try to up the ante and play a bit better than the night before. It was essential to measure your performance by your own yardstick, but it was difficult to remain so focused. I remember one night, I thought the sound was terrible and I got a bit of a mood on, and really didn't engage in the way I normally would, but Matt cut me short on that. Matt doesn't like conflict of any sort, but after that gig I remembering him handing out our wages at the hotel, and he stared hard at me and said "I pay you to make me sound good". That was all, but it really struck me. I realised that he wanted me to perform a specific role, but also to break free and be inspired, so I had to carefully manage that double-edged sword to do my job properly.

'Those three years I spent with the Matt Taylor Band made me a much better player. It really taught me to reign things in, to be more disciplined in my performances. It becomes the total focus of my day. I'm preparing myself for that night's gig from 7.30am, figuring out what clothes to wear, going through what songs I'll play – even if I've played them all before at the previous gig. But I can't plan it all out in A-Z fashion, because there has to be room for inspiration to come in.'

Friendships formed during Chris' many years of touring have been especially important, as the camaraderie extends far beyond music. 'I really can't remember when Chris and I first met, because it's like he has always been there with me,' says Matt Taylor. 'We share so much – the same love of music, the same love of classic British comedy. The hours fly by whenever we get together. Being with Chris and making music with him has been such a positive part of my life.'

Chris is grateful for Matt's generosity while they were on tour – especially when he paid for Chris to enjoy a joyflight over Burleigh Heads, Queensland, aboard an open-cockpit Tiger Moth bi-plane piloted by Bruce McGarvey. 'Matt knows how much I love aviation, and that flight was the greatest thrill for me.'

Chris especially treasures his enduring friendship with Phil Manning, who often forgoes booked hotel accommodation when he comes into Adelaide to instead say at Chris's home, sharing lengthy conversations about politics, current affairs, humour and their love of old films. 'I call it The Rescue – being able to extend a home and a cooked meal and some easy companionship to a muso on the road,' says Chris. 'It has certainly been a saving grace offered to me when I'm out on tour. It's an important way we can look after each other.'

Their lives have intertwined so much as musicians since the early 1970s – especially through both having had stints in Chain as lead guitarist. Chris even filled in for Phil for a Chain gig at very short notice, flying into Alice Springs so that Phil could race back to Melbourne when his wife went into labour (Phil just made it into the delivery theatre for the birth of their son).

Phil notes that when listening back to tapes of them performing together on stage and exchanging lines during solos, he often can't tell who is playing what part, such is the similarity of their guitar vocabulary and ability to read and react to each musical moment.

'Phil was my biggest Australian influence as a guitarist,' says Chris. 'When I first came to Australia, I'd go to hear Phil play in the earliest version of Chain, when Wendy Saddington was the singer, and he was one of the first guitar players to befriend me and invite me to join him on stage. His tone was phenomenal, his phrasing fantastic, and he always played with such great taste and intent. He'd play early Fleetwood Mac songs and it was the closest you'd get to seeing Peter Green perform live. What he did on stage provided a template of what I wanted to achieve and what I wanted to be like as a musician.'

So, what does Phil think is special about Chris's playing? 'Well, he's basically a lunatic,' Phil says before erupting into a hail of laughter. 'I love that there's so much humour in Chris's playing. He always puts his personality across when he plays the guitar, in very adventurous ways. His openness to all styles of music comes out in his playing; he can be peeling off a John Lee Hooker groove and then introduce Ravi Shankar phrases to it – and he pulls it off! I can't think of many others who would even have the audacity to think of that, let alone succeed. That's just one of the reasons why I think he's very special.'

Many of Chris's special moments have been captured on a league of recordings – from live concerts to home demos and studio recordings. Each mode requires a different set of skills and approaches, with close attention needing to be paid to all the variables in play: the size and acoustics of the rooms in question, and how that will affect the sound of what you play and how you perform your songs.

'Home demos are the sketch pad before the painting and provide a good template on which to try different ideas and figure out arrangements,' says Chris.

However, booking time in a recording studio presents a unique opportunity to be creative. 'It's so much more than just capturing a live performance,' Chris explains. 'You can have complete arrangements, or a handful of half-written preparations, or simply react in the moment and make it all up on the spot. I've found that all of these approaches have their place in the recording studio, and they certainly provide a wide variety of musical flavours, but while I greatly respect structured composition, I really love improvisation. As the great Sir Peter Ustinov once said, improvisation is nothing more than thinking aloud.

'The recording studio allows you the opportunity to record your music in layers via the process of overdubbing – thank God for the genius of Les Paul – but when you do this, your timing has to be accurate. If you have the discipline to get it right, you can build up the most fabulous layers of harmony, creating wonderful ambience and lushness in the sound while you're having fun mixing the track.'

Patience during the recording process brings its own rewards. 'When I was younger, I'd want to finish everything in the one session, but I've learned that if you give yourself time, you end up with a more measured assessment of your music. Long sessions in the studio bring fatigue, so sometimes you just have to take a break to clean out your brain and your ears. It's the same when you're working with engineers on the final mix of a song; you need to take the time to hear the finished version through a wide variety of different speaker systems. It's such a difficult process, because a mixer can either help or destroy your music.

'I've always been grateful to have skilled help, but ultimately I have to shape a clear idea of what I want. A skilled engineer will understand what I'm trying to achieve, so you then have to work as a team to thrash out a successful outcome.'

Chris's many invitations to play instruments on other people's records have brought countless interesting and challenging moments – not only playing acoustic and electric guitars, but also banjo, bass, percussion and a vast array of different ethnic musical instruments. 'I get asked to participate because they like what I do, but then I realise it's my job to not just do whatever I want, but to provide something that will enhance the colour of their music.

'My only request of them is that if I play a guitar solo, please don't cut it up and edit it, because I have always devised a purposeful beginning, middle and end to the piece. If time permits in the studio, I'll often provide three different solos for them to choose from. But I really want each solo to stand alone. I view it like a well-written phrase or paragraph in a book; if you mess around with them, their meaning and emotional core will be lost.'

Sometimes, the sessions don't quite unfold as planned. 'I was asked to play bottleneck slide guitar for an advertisement to promote an American play, so I got my guitar out, tuned it and noodled around on the fretboard. After about two minutes, the recording engineer told me he had everything that he needed. What? I was only warming up! Oh well, I still got a nice pay cheque a few weeks later.'

Chris also enjoys composing and recording music for film and cartoon soundtracks, and dance company performances. 'I was so thrilled that one of these films won the best young film makers' award in South Australia, and a cartoon was nominated for a Best Soundtrack award at the Cannes Film Festival in France and the Woodstock Film Festival in the US.

'While I can't dance because I've got two left feet, I love providing the music that can support the graceful movement of skilled dancers that remind us of the miracle of the human body.'

Friendships form the basis of various musical outfits dotted around Australia that Chris has sporadically slipped into.

National Collection was a blues/rock trio built from Chris's friendship with Melbourne bass player Peter Howell that became an especially popular act in Tasmania. 'Drummer Robin Andrews (now sadly deceased) came from Devonport in northern Tasmania and he had played with Normie Rowe, Phil Manning and many others,' explains Chris. 'He was the link that got us in front of a very loyal Tasmanian audience. We did 17 tours of the island through the late-1980s.'

This included meeting an enthusiastic punter at a St Helens gig who was a helicopter pilot, and he exchanged a guitar lesson from Chris in return for a joy flight in his chopper over the local beaches. The band also set the record amount spent over the bar during a gig at the DogHouse venue in Hobart. 'We found bottles of champagne and thank you notes from the venue management on our amplifiers the next morning,' remembers Chris. However, they also had a disgruntled former band member placing banners declaring 'GIG CANCELLED' over National Collection posters promoting a Launceston Hotel gig, which went ahead regardless to a large and enthusiastic crowd.

Chris's enthusiasm for playing in Tasmania extended to being involved in an all-night radio session. Having already played three gigs in the one night at venues across Hobart, Chris went to a local radio station and was invited by the announcer to do an on-air, impromptu acoustic blues concert. Listeners began ringing into the station and requesting more songs from Chris. 'One guy had walked for 25 minutes to reach a public phone box to call in his request, but then asked me to wait for another 25 minutes before I performed it, so that he could make it home to hear it on his radio.' Chris's live-to-air performance marathon went on until 4am.

Even Tasmania's notorious rain couldn't dampen Chris's spirits. Once, he had to share a bedroom with bass player Frank Lang in the Billabong Hotel. 'Frank is a very solidly built man and he had the top bunk in a very small room, and during the night, very loud snoring started – and continued all through the early hours. By 3am, I decided that the only sensible thing for me to do was go out walking, but when I was at the furthest point from the hotel, it began pouring with rain. The local radio station had its music piped through speakers on posts along the street, and as I stood there getting absolutely soaked, I was serenaded by Louis Armstrong singing *Wonderful World*. I couldn't help but laugh my head off. The irony of that situation was not lost on me.'

The joyous reception that Chris kept receiving in Tasmania was being replicated in many other parts of the nation. 'Building up a reputation in different parts of Australia gave me more opportunities, more touring with lots of different outfits, and it led to a strong following for my music in many cities.'

Playing in Sydney holds some strong memories for Chris, from late-night jam sessions in the Manzil Room (the infamous all-hours musician's hangout in King's Cross), to the Harbour View Hotel, playing as an electric trio with bass player Dirk DuBois and former Kevin Borich Express drummer John Annis, and using a radio transmitter on his guitar to burst into the street beside the pub for a howling slide guitar solo unleashed before some bewildered pedestrians. He also remembers some startling open-air gigs performed by fusion band Indian Pacific in The Rocks beside Sydney Harbour, and at Taronga Park Zoo.

Touring brought a few opportunities that combined Chris's primary loves of aviation, music and family. While playing gigs in Melbourne, Chris connected with his friend Rick Banfield, who flew Chris in his white Bell 47 helicopter down to Phillip Island for a surprise visit to his mother, with Chris's two guitar cases placed inside the stretcher panniers on either side of the helicopter's passenger cabin. 'We flew a couple of circuits around my mother's house, then landed at the airport and rang my mum to casually inform her that we were about to pop around for a cup of tea. She almost keeled over.'

However, touring has also taken a serious toll on Chris's health. Two accidents in cars while travelling between gigs have left him with a severely damaged back. The first was in 1986, when he was touring around rural South Australia with The Others. A re-tread tyre on the van burst, on the highway outside of Snowtown, the vehicle rolled over and the wreck was left to rust beside the highway. Fortunately, the passengers were able to walk away from the accident. 'We were probably lucky to get out of it intact, but I got thrown around quite a bit and only realised much later that my back had been seriously hurt.'

The other accident happened in Tasmania, travelling with National Collection in the late-1980s. 'Our van went into the gravel, and then into a paddock at a fair speed, and the van rolled. Everything got wrecked, including a hired PA system that we had brought with us from Adelaide. It was a disaster. Soon afterwards, we had to organise another tour of Tasmania, so we could earn enough money to pay for all the damage. I was so concerned about getting our debt sorted out that I didn't get myself checked out thoroughly, because I'd done even more damage to my back.

'Those two accidents really shook me around. I really didn't want to go back to travelling long distances by car when we went on tour. I doubted that my back would be able to stand up to a 14-hour stint in a car. I'd always try to fly to other cities, even though it often meant the rest of the band went by road with all the equipment. It certainly wasn't ideal, but it was the only way I could get to a gig in a satisfactory shape to play.'

This underlines Chris's firm belief that the show must go on. 'Sometimes the circumstances surrounding a gig may not be ideal, but when you walk out onto a stage, you have to be focused, energised and ready to entertain your audience. I've done shows when I'm ill, but still manage to pull off a convincing performance,' he says. 'If my throat's sore, I'll start narrating the lyrics rather than trying to sing, and maybe play longer improvised instrumental passages. Anything to make it work.

'I really regret that I've had to cancel some shows due to chronic back pain leaving me unable to walk. I don't like to let anyone down.'

Despite such limits, fresh opportunities have continually come Chris's way. A friend who was living in Darwin invited Chris to travel to the Top End for a weekend of gigs in the early 1990s, and this led to the foundation of a devoted fan base that has seen Chris make 13 subsequent visits to Darwin. Only two of those visits occurred during the wet season, and Chris learned the hard way that humidity caused by the monsoon rains is especially punishing on musical instruments. The phenomenal amount of moisture in the air warped the body of his favourite 12-string guitar (first owned by Phil Manning, then Jeff Lang, before it came to Chris). 'I went to get it repaired and the locals just laughed at me, asking why the hell I had brought a treasured guitar up to Darwin in the wet season. That was all the help they had to offer.'

Another big learning curve about playing gigs up north was to accept the very casual timetable that dictated how performances were staged. 'I remember arriving for a workshop gig at NT University, and it became clear that no-one cared very much about being punctual,' says Chris, 'and that was a real jolt to me. It's not how I operate. I got there promptly and set up my gear, but there was no PA system on the stage. It got to the scheduled playing time of 1.30pm, and there was still no PA, and the audience only just started to straggle in by about a quarter to two. I asked what the hell was going on and was informed 'Don't worry mate. We're on Darwin time. The PA will eventually get here.' And it did. Nobody but me seemed at all concerned about it. I really had to get my head around the fact nobody else gave a fuck about being punctual. Oh well. When in Rome, make like a Roman.'

Sometimes, it wasn't easy for Chris to win the attention of a Darwin audience. 'I played an open-air gig at Fred's Pass, doing a solo acoustic set on a stage located at one side of a vast oval, and the entire crowd squeezed into the beer tent on the other side of the oval. During my last song, I unplugged and walked across the oval, still singing and strumming, went into the tent and ordered a beer, drank it while I kept playing one-handed, then finished the song to a rousing ovation and had everyone keen to keep buying me beers and chatting.'

Chris marks each of his Darwin visits by going to the Mindi Beach markets and buying a painted gecko figurine – which now form a long, colourful procession of a dozen geckos, fixed onto the ceiling of his lounge room at home in Seaford Rise, Adelaide. 'I also remember one open-air gig down by the beach at Fanny Bay, when a rather large monitor lizard casually strolled in front of me across the stage,' he says. 'Sure, I often ask the sound engineer for more monitor, but that was ridiculous!'

When he ventures north, Chris picks up a band of local players to perform with him on stage, affectionately called the Darwin Blues Boys. 'The Darwin shows were all done on a shoestring, so the financial constrains meant I was never able to bring my own band with me. I would arrive two days before the first show and rehearse with whoever was available.' Sometimes, a few of the local Darwin musos were wary of this bespectacled outsider stepping into their domain. 'It was a bit like an animal straying into a rival's territory. There was an element of having to prove myself before I got accepted.'

Chris obviously passed the test, and quickly made a positive impression on Darwin audiences. 'After one of those early gigs, a guy bowled up to me and said "You're sick" and I replied "No, I'm actually quite well, thank you." It was the first time I'd heard that terminology and had no idea he was trying to give me compliment.'

It only took a few gigs before Chris was heralded as a local favourite, and he built a loyal Darwin following in a similar way to how National Collection had amassed a parochial fan base in Tasmania. 'It worked out very nicely for me to be regarded as flavour-of-the-moment for about four years in Darwin.'

The Melbourne Blues Disciples formed through Chris's close association with musicians who had played for many years with Dutch Tilders. After Dutch died in April 2011, his former band colleagues – guitarist Greg Dodd, drummer Winston Galea and bass player Peter Beulke – invited Chris to join them for an initial round of gigs in Melbourne, then wider bouts of occasional touring. Chris whimsically suggested the band name over the phone, which Greg Dodd enthusiastically embraced and began promoting. They would regularly come together to perform at the annual Blues For Lost Souls concert, a benefit for homeless people that also featured other Dutch Tilders associates, including guitarist Geoff Achison. 'It was so lovely to go to Melbourne and play music with those guys, but it was never designed to be a continuation of the Dutch Tilders Band,' says Chris. 'It was entirely separate.' While the Melbourne Blues Disciples haven't performed together since 2016, with Dodd currently working and living overseas, Chris explains that the band 'is only in recess at the moment'.

A more recent performance relationship has developed between Chris and 8-Ball Aitken, the 40-year-old swampy blues guitar player from Brisbane. While they seem poles apart, in the tone of their different musical styles and with the space of a generation between them, Chris says it's their differences that have helped cement a very strong friendship. 'We each bring something quite different to the table whenever we play, and that adds colours to our performance that would otherwise be missing,' explains Chris.

They first came together at blues festivals after 8-Ball emerged as a new star attraction in 2006, famed for building his slide guitar out of an old metal Tim Tam biscuit tin. Impressed with Chris's own frenetic guitar solos, 8-Ball invited Chris to jam with him on stage, and Chris returned the favour during his own sets. Soon after, Chris invited 8-Ball to stay at his Seaford Rise home when the Queenslander came to Adelaide for gigs, and their friendship grew over late-night meals and lengthy conversations. 'His enthusiasm is so infectious,' says Chris, 'and he's such a keen student of blues. He's now got it into his head that more people need to be schooled in Australia's older generation of blues guitarists, and has been one of my greatest supporters ever since.'

8-Ball Aitken has invited Chris to accompany him at gigs in Brisbane, which served as Chris's important re-introduction to the Queensland blues scene and led to frequent tours with 8-Ball Aitken's backing band.

Lasting friendships have also extended to many people in the cities where Chris visits. 'The people who I meet at gigs often become my tour guides the following morning. I go on tour with the notion that if I'm going to visit someone's else's town, I'm going to learn something about it. I'd get people to show me the things they're most proud of, or that they find most interesting about their town. I collect souvenirs and brochures, buy books, eat at the locals' favourite restaurants, and I've built up a vivid understanding about so many places around Australia. Then I get to tell other people – especially musicians from other countries who I meet – about the places I've been to. When I was touring, I was never an empty vessel. I'd always take in as much as I'd give.'

Tour... record... tour

Sometimes when I feel I want to give it all away and close the last page in my book
Somewhere deep inside me that same old voice begins to say
'Come on Chris, have yourself another look'
Because you're always gonna find somebody who's got it worse than you
Don't matter how much you think you've got the blues
And I wish that I could help somebody else
so much more than I ever seem to do.

Feelings, by Chris Finnen, 1978

There have also been extraordinary incidents on the road that have shaken Chris. He remembers a tour to Brisbane, when he was playing at The Healer nightclub in Fortitude Valley. He had just finished a typically epic and joyous version of *African Marketplace* and was heading to the dressing room for a break between sets, when he noticed an ambulance crew race into the building. 'I found out that a woman had died on the dance floor. She came along to our shows every time we played at this club in Brisbane. I thought about what had happened for months after the show, at first with great sadness, but then I began to realise there was a fragile beauty to the moment – that someone dancing to music which brought them great joy was then offered a quick exit. There are far more unpleasant ways to go out.'

Ultimately, the long road of recording and performing has resulted in fulsome peer and public recognition. Chris was inducted into the SA Music Hall of Fame in 1995, and nominated for a Pride of Australia medal in 2013, for his work in community and mentoring.

'When I was a kid, I felt quite insecure and believed that I just didn't fit in, so to receive an award comes as a wonderful approval of my work. It's a reward for hard work. I'm proud of every award I've received, because they illustrate the journey I've been on, from being that insecure kid to a happy adult.'

A surprise came in August 2013, when Chris was inducted into the Blues Hall of Fame: Australia – a virtual organisation that cited

Chris as a 'Great Blues Artist' (the first of three tiers of recognition by this organisation). The person who provided access to this citation was New York blues guitarist John Earl Walker, who had commenced a relationship with Barossa Valley-based blues radio presenter Tess Coleman. After Tess had visited Walker in New York, he came visit to Adelaide in July 2006. 'I wanted to connect with local musicians and Tess recommended that I meet Chris Finnen,' says Walker, who is currently living in Florida, 'so I went to see him play at the Semaphore Workers Club and sat in with him on a few songs. We hit it off musically and formed a friendship right away.'

In 2012, Walker was inducted into the New York Blues Hall of Fame (entirely separate from the Blues Hall of Fame in Memphis), which says on its website (blueshalloffame.com) is dedicated to honouring, showcasing and inducting all of the great blues artists of the world. Walker was also made an ambassador for the organisation and encouraged, as a regular visitor to Australia, to stimulate an Australia Blues Hall of Fame.

'I never asked or wanted to be an ambassador, but I did do one induction ceremony at a blues festival in 2013, where I inducted Chris into the Australian Blues Hall of Fame,' says Walker, 'because I absolutely believe that he fills the criteria.'

This award coincided with the floodgates opening for further recognition of Chris at home during 2014 – being inducted into the Adelaide Music Collective Hall of Fame, winning Derringers Music Blues Awards Outstanding Instrumentalist, and being honoured as patron of the South Australian Roots and Blues Association. 'You only get something if you've earned it, and I'm proud to say I've put a lifetime's work into the music that led to these awards.'

In 2018, Chris received the Paul Hay Award, recognising his outstanding service to South Australian Roots and Blues Music, and named in honour of the late Adelaide blues musician. Of all the awards he has received, Chris says this means the most to him. 'Paul Hay was a wonderful friend – we called him Froggy – and he was a joy to be around. Playing music with him was always inspirational and I enjoyed recording three CDs with him – his solo album called *Together*, and two with his band Rhumboogie. Losing him was so painful, but my happy memories of Froggy come back every time I see this award.'

Chris also takes delight in recognising others, and loves the opportunity to present awards to fellow musicians. 'I've had the opportunity to present an award to my dear friend Gwyn Ashton, who is one of the most hard-working and dedicated musicians to present Australian music both here and abroad. He has a staggering songwriting output, and spends so many long hours travelling in a van on the road to keep playing gig after gig. Presenting an award to Gwyn marked a significant achievement, and certainly was not a mere token. When I perform with Gwyn, I think of it as the amalgamation of two men dedicated to their musical journeys who happily come together to try and break some new ground.'

Now, after celebrating his 70th birthday, Chris reflects on having made it through a tumultuous journey as a musician – mindful that many of his contemporaries, colleagues and dearest friends are no longer alive. He's paid attention to the pitfalls and foibles that consumed too many good people.

'There have been times over the years when I've been too drunk, too stoned, but I soon learned to temper my behaviour. Being on the cusp of having Type-2 diabetes certainly made me calm down, and it's been about 25 years since I've consumed drugs, because that's not the path I wanted to go down. I've always been conscious of my health. Because I love food, I've always eaten well and enjoyed a varied diet. Because I don't drive a car, I've always done a lot of walking, so I've had a regular exercise regime. But, having said that, perhaps I should have learned about the concept of moderation a few years earlier...'

I have made many wonderful friends through 50 years of playing music, and to list them all would require another book.

Most of the musicians I've met have been kind, interesting people. Sure, there has been one or two egotists among them, plus various opportunists, coat-tail riders or just plain fucking idiots, but 95% of them have been and are still are great people.

There are a few I must thank. My earliest and deepest influences during the 1960s and early 1970s were provided by Phil Manning, Lobby Loyde, Mick Jurd, Billy Thorpe, Chris Stockley, Ross Hannaford, Barry Harvey, Barry Sullivan, Warren Morgan, Doug Ford and Matt Taylor. As a teenager, I remember listening to Phil Manning's immaculate tone, phrasing and musical ideas, which helped me to focus on what I should do. This was far different to what I taught myself by listening to records, because I would talk to Phil and ask him so many questions – and then I'd hear him play the same song a week later with a new twist and some fresh ideas added, and my line of enquiry would start again. This was such a big help to me.

Lobby Loyde was very different – mind-blowingly loud, playing a lot of notes and always with his finger on the guitar's tremolo bar. This man developed his own distinctive style, and the gigs he played with the Wild Cherries and Billy Thorpe were the best performances I ever heard him do.

Mick Jurd and myself became very good friends and played many gigs together in Adelaide. I first heard him play in Levi Smith Clefts with Barry McAskill and Bruce Howe, when they first visited Melbourne. I will always remember Mick's beautiful instrumental *Relief From a Lighted Doorway*, notable for his delicate use of volume control on his white Fender Stratocaster guitar.

Ross Hannaford stands out on his own. He was a wizard in the use of chords and his ideas were so individual, so well executed, so subtle and so effective. His stage presence was always so joyful and his tone so listenable.

Chris Stockley was another chord wizard. I used to really enjoy him playing the song *Nashville Cats* on his Gibson SG guitar when he was in Axiom.

The Australian vocalists who moved me during this formative era included Gerry Humphreys, Matt Taylor, Barry McAskill, Wendy Saddington, Margret RoadKnight, Kerry Biddell, Max Merritt and Jeff St John. All of them had something very personal to give in their performances, and all of them committed to always give 100%.

I also need to mention a few South Australian guitarists that I admire. On the acoustic guitar, Cal Williams Jnr has shown a work ethic and commitment to playing, performing and teaching that provides benefits for everybody.

Up-and-coming younger electric guitar players Stefan Hauk and the hard-working Dusty Lee Stephenson offer a good, positive pathway to the future. And my favourite South Australian guitarist Nick Kipridis has imagination and individuality that is truly inspiring. He takes the listener on a journey that is full of joy – and this encourages you to try and play guitar a little better.

The list of musicians who have inspired me could go on and on, with all manner of drummers, horn players, bass players, keyboard players and more. But what this recollection points to is that all these people were key players and pioneers who were instrumental in shaping the early sound of Australian rhythm and blues. I joined them in taking music from other countries and reshaping it, as we learned to play in a way that is truly our own. These people showed everyone the way forward.

Finnenisms

We have all given a lot to Australian blues – and it gives a lot back to us. Therefore, it feels so good to have been a part of an epic journey, from close to the beginning of blues being played in this country, to now understanding that I now have a duty to pass it all on. This music is ours. Long may we all celebrate it.

A final note . . .
by Jeff Lang

As Chris and I became fast friends, he extended an open invitation for me to stay in the spare room at his home when I came through Adelaide, and it was on these subsequent visits that I became aware just how broad Chris' range of influence is. My musical diet diversified rapidly with every trip to Adelaide, as Chris frequently reached into the massive collection of LPs that covered an entire wall in his lounge room to grab a copy of an album by Dollar Brand, or Larry Coryell, Blind Blake, David Lindley, and countless others, saying 'Oh, you have to hear this . . .' And he was always right – I *did* have to hear whichever record he played. His enthusiasm for music was childlike, in the best sense, and utterly infectious.

He showed me, by example, a way to be when you're in love with music. I always felt that for Chris, music was something simultaneously sacred yet elemental, central to his sense of place in the world, and it's a feeling that I share. It's as though he feels a bond with humanity through his love for music.

We came together for performances many times over the years, some with him as a guest at my Adelaide shows, and then we toured around the country together in a van, playing double-billed gigs, where we'd do a set separately, then perform one together. He said to me early on that you can learn so much about a person from the way they play – their sense of humour, the intensity of their passion, their temperament – especially on an instrument which can be prone to hogging the sonic highway like the guitar. A person's capacity to listen and their willingness to engage in a meaningful exchange of ideas becomes quite apparent in the musical conversations that happen when guitarists jam with each other. Chris always gave more than he took and I never failed to learn something new during our nightly exchanges on stage.

One consistent factor is that Chris Finnen never merely dials in his show. He always reaches for something which can lift the spirits of whoever is present in the room. I've seen him make people weep with joy, myself included, as he plays *African Marketplace* on solo electric guitar, with his head swaying from side to side, completely inside the music, pulling us all along with him as he took flight.

When I hosted a series of late-night sessions as part of the first Adelaide International Guitar Festival in 2007, I had the opportunity to invite other players to sit in with me and my band, and Chris was one of those I wanted to take part. The night Chris sat in with us, the brilliant American guitarist Vernon Reid was also going to play. He had the biggest grin on his face when he described watching Chris play with us. 'This little guy with glasses on gets up with a Stratocaster and the first thing he does when the song starts was to turn it over and start *playing the springs* in the back of the tremolo cavity!' He started laughing and went on to say, 'I thought "Now this is my kinda guy – he's a madman!"' That's the effect Chris has on people. It's such a joy.

I love Chris like a dear family member, and he's been a massive influence on me as well as a source of inspiration. It's his spirit – it's authentic, pure, mischievous and daring. We need people like this around, but there's only one Chris Finnen.

Jeff Lang,
February 2024

Chris Finnen Discography

Original recordings

- *The Journey/Dream Suite*, Chris Finnen (solo) – 1978
- *Real Australian Blues: Volume Two* (compilation album) – 1993
- *Deep South: South Australian Rhythm and Blues* (compilation album) – 1994
- *The Chris Finnen Blues Band: Live* – 1994, Exile Records
- *Exile Records Guitar Sampler*, Chris Finnen with Mal Eastick, Danny Gatton and the Hellcasters – 1995, Exile Records
- *Finnen and Lang Live at The Vineyard*, Chris Finnen with Jeff Lang – 1996, The Crossing Record Company
- *Three Sixty Degrees*, Chris Finnen – 1997, The Crossing Record Company
- *From the Kitchen Table ... To the Bottom of the Morning*, Chris Finnen – 1998, The Crossing Record Company
- *Live at the Singing Gallery*, Chris Finnen – 2000
- *Strings and Sticks*, Chris Finnen – 2006, limited independent release
- *Electric Number One*, Chris Finnen Band – 2006
- *Building Musical Bridges Between Cultures: Singing Gallery Sessions Live*, Chris Finnen – 2007, double DVD
- *Blues and Beyond*, Chris Finnen – 2012
- *Ali Kat Guitar Boogie Shuffle*, Chris Finnen – 2014
- *To My Southern Town*, Chris Finnen Band – 2020
- *Live in Lockdown 2020*, Chris Finnen Band – 2020, DVD

Recording collaborations and guest sessions

- *Always Land on Your Feet*, Matt Taylor Band – 1982, vinyl, cassette, DVD
- *Your Voice Within Me*, Indian Pacific – 1989
- *Rainbow Fire*, Indian Pacific – 1991
- *Australian Sihk Rhythm and Soul*, Dya Singh – 1993
- *Fringe Benefits*, Margret RoadKnight – 1993
- *Pilgrim*, Dya Singh – 1996
- *Native Dog Creek*, Jeff Lang – 1996
- *Introducing Michael Brown*, Michael Brown – 1996
- *Don't Tell Frank*, Hoy-Hoy! – 1996
- *Restless*, Peter David Hale – 1996

- *Blue Jay,* Blue Jay – 1997
- *Woodford Blues Experience* – 1998
- *1998 Gympie Muster Collection* – 1998
- *Down Under the Blues,* Mike Festa – 1998
- *Starting Over,* The Brown Brothers – 1999
- *When Love Comes to You,* Leigh Marshall – 1999
- *Perceptions,* Sebastian Punitham – 1999
- *The Effects of Curry,* Finnen and Fraser – 2001
- *River of Songs: From the Mountains of Bhutan to the Oceans of Australia,* Lhamo Dukpa – 2005
- *Hoy-Hoy! 18th Birthday Show,* Hoy-Hoy! – 2005, CD + DVD
- *A Portrait,* Leigh Marshall – 2007
- *Threads,* Linda Rankin – 2007
- *Various People* – 2007
- *You Gotta Learn to Rhumboogie,* Rhumboogie – 2008
- *Fleurieu Folk Festival Highlights* – 2009, DVD
- *It's All Good,* Linda Rankin – 2010
- *Dutch Tilders and Friends: Cancer Benefit Concert* – 2010, DVD
- *Living in the Curlew Republic,* Colin Offord – 2012
- *Fanbdabidozi,* Rhumboogie – 2014
- *Together,* Paul Hay – 2014
- *Hoy-Hoy! Farewell Concert,* Hoy-Hoy! – 2014, DVD
- *Goading the Beast,* Colin Offord – 2015, 5CD set + DVD
- *Weeping Spell,* Chris Finnen with Kory Horwood and Cal Williams Jnr – 2016
- *Winter Done,* Cal Williams Jnr and Kory Horwood – 2016
- *Dreams Enough to Share,* The Fatherhood – 2016
- *Yesterday's Heroes: Album Launch Concert* – 2016, DVD
- *Ragas, Jugs and Mojo Hands,* Gwyn Ashton, Chris Finnen and Peter Beulke – 2016
- *Off the Cuff,* Jay Hoad and Chris Finnen – 2016
- *Red Moon,* Leigh Marshall – 2018
- *Ear To Ear,* Love Grins – 2019
- *There to Now,* Linda Rankin and Allye Sincliar – 2019
- *Michael Wehrs with Chris Finnen* – 2021
- *Time Distance Music,* Colin Offord – 2023

Chris Finnen References and biographies in published books

- *Who's Who of Australian Rock: Third Edition,* compiled by Chris Spencer and Zbig Nowara – 1993
- *The Encyclopedia of Australian Rock and Pop,* Ian McFarlane – 1999
- *Shooting Stars: Anecdotes of a Videographer,* Jethro Heller – 2020
- *Blues Portrait: A Profile of the Australian Blues Scene, Volume* 2, Pauline Bailey – 2021

Music awards and accolades

- SAMIA: Most Outstanding Contribution to the Blues – 1994
- Australian Music Awards @ Lithgow Blues Music Festival, Best Guitarist – 1995
- Australian Music Awards @ Lithgow Blues Music Festival, Best New Band – 1995
- SAMIA: Hall of Fame Award – 1995
- SAMIA: Most Outstanding Guitarist of the Year – 1995
- SAMIA: Most Outstanding Guitarist of the Year – 1996
- SAMIA: Most Outstanding Guitarist of the Year – 1997
- SAMIA: Most Outstanding Guitarist of the Year – 1998
- South Australian Blues Society: Life Member – 1998
- Gouldburn Blues Music (Chain) Awards, Song of the Year – 1999
- Gouldburn Blues Music (Chain) Awards, Album of the Year – 1999
- Gouldburn Blues Music (Chain) Awards, Male Vocalist of the Year – 1999
- SA Folk Awards: Best Contribution to Contemporary Music in South Australia – 1999
- American Heritage Blues Hall of Fame, New York, USA: Great Blues Artist – 2013
- Pride of Australia Medal: For Community Work Through Music – 2013
- AMC Music Hall of Fame – 2014
- Made a patron of Adelaide Roots and Blues Association – 2014
- Derringers Music Blues Awards: Outstanding Instrumentalist – 2014
- Adelaide Roots and Blues Association: Album of the Year – 2016
- ARBA Paul Hay Award: Outstanding Service to Blues – 2018
- Ambassador of Port Noarlunga Blues Festival – 2018
- Adelaide Roots and Blues Association: Album of the Year – 2021

'The guitar is a voice, not just a guitar.
Feel it, breathe it. Make it sing.'

Chris Finnen

Wakefield Press is an independent publishing and
distribution company based in Adelaide, South Australia.
We love good stories and publish beautiful books.
To see our full range of books, please visit our website at
www.wakefieldpress.com.au
where all titles are available for purchase.
To keep up with our latest releases, news and events,
subscribe to our monthly newsletter.

Find us!

Facebook: www.facebook.com/wakefield.press
Twitter: www.twitter.com/wakefieldpress
Instagram: www.instagram.com/wakefieldpress

www.ingramcontent.com/pod-product-compliance
Lightning Source LLC
Chambersburg PA
CBHW061248230426
43663CB00021B/2939